101 THINGS EVERYONE SHOULD KNOW ABOUT CATHOLICISM

Beliefs, Practices, Customs, and Traditions

6/05

Published by Adams Media,
an F+W Publications Company
57 Littlefield Street
Avon, MA 02322
www.adamsmedia.com

ISBN: 1-59337-266-3

Printed in Canada

J I H G F E D C B A

Keeler, Helen.
101 things everyone should know about Catholicism /
by Helen Keeler and Susan Grimbly ; edited by James B. Wiggins.
p.   cm.
ISBN 1-59337-266-3
1. Catholic Church--Doctrines. 2. Catholic Church--Customs and practices.
I. Title: One hundred one things everyone should know about Catholicism.
II. Title: One hundred and one things everyone should know about Catholicism.
III. Grimbly, Susan. IV. Wiggins, James B. V. Title.
BX1754.K324   2005
282--dc22   2004013574

Contents

INTRODUCTION

There may be as many as 2 billion Christians in the world today. Among the major groupings, the Roman Catholic Church has nearly a billion members, compared to about 800 million Protestants of all denominations and 200 million members of Eastern Orthodox Churches. Roman Catholicism's influence extends to every continent and most nations of the world.

The Bishop of Rome, more commonly known as the pope, leads the Church. The pope's leadership is unique, in that he presides not only over the Roman Catholic Church, but over the Vatican—an independent nation—as well. Thus, in interacting with heads of state and also with leaders of other religious traditions, the pope has access to some of the most important decision-makers in the world. The pope's prominence, and that of the Church he leads, took centuries to develop. The story of the Roman Catholic Church's development is one of epic proportions. Its story is inseparable from the story of Western civilization since the first century A.D. In fact, as you will soon find in the pages of this text, the Western world's advancement has depended upon some of the great events, figures, and thinkers of the Church.

In the Catholic faith, the primacy of the Bishop of Rome dates back all the way to the early days following Jesus' death and the Resurrection. The Church teaches that St. Peter was the first Bishop of Rome. As such, the link between God's acts, made present in the life and teachings of Jesus, remains unbroken through the chain of leaders that has followed from St. Peter, through the centuries until now. This chain of transmitting the authentic understanding of who Jesus was—the only begotten Son of God the Father—and what His message was, as conveyed in the Apostles' and Nicene Creeds, is called "apostolic succession."

As the chief authority in the Roman Catholic Church, the pope stands at the pinnacle of Church hierarchy and authority. But the pope is not the sole figure of authority in the Church. At the next level below him comes the cardinal of bishops, followed by the provincial bishops, then priests. Church bishops collectively convene from time to time in councils to make decisions on pressing matters. And, in rare cases, the pope makes pronouncements on matters of faith or morals that the Roman Catholic Church views as infallible and binding on all its members.

The Church's hierarchy has been in place for centuries, but this ruling body is far from stagnant. The Roman Catholic Church was sometimes reluctant to change in centuries past, but since the days of the Second Vatican Council in the mid-twentieth century, the Church has continued to move forward as an evolving, dynamic entity striving to adjust to contemporary times. Consider laity involvement, for instance. Though lay people are at the base of the Church's hierarchical pyramid, they are far from unimportant. While traditionally the laity had less say in matters of the Church, that is changing. The Catholic faith is rooted in a strong belief in the power of faith and good works and, indeed, today's lay community is actively seeking ways to expand its role in both of those areas. Catholics are becoming more involved in parish life, participating in the Mass (the Catholic service of worship) to a greater degree, and ministering to the community around them. And, although

Roman Catholicism has historically been a highly patriarchal institution, even that is slowly changing today, as women also take on a greater participatory role within the Church. (At present, the question of female ordination remains a hot topic.)

Roman Catholicism is a faith full of unique practices, customs, and traditions. Among its most distinctive facets are the rituals called sacraments. Sacraments are defined as outward and visible signs of inward grace, which the Church makes available for the salvation of those who receive them. There are seven of them, each marking a major moment in a Catholic's life. The Catholic faith teaches that Jesus created the Church to be the mediator between God and humans, and the sacraments are the means by which God's grace continues to be available to humanity. Because Roman Catholicism provides these rituals, the church itself is highly valued, so much so that for centuries it has been proclaimed that "outside the church, no salvation."

The sense of confidence that the Roman Catholic Church engenders in its members is one of its great strengths. Firmly declaring that it exists as the embodiment of God's message and the means of providing a saving relationship for humans with God, Roman Catholicism has taken its message around the globe and attracted millions of adherents.

In this book, you'll glean a basic understanding of this rich religious tradition, its history, essential teachings and beliefs, views on the Scriptures, and primary rituals. You'll also get a glimpse of the Church's role in contemporary society, as the Church continues to forge ahead in the new millennium.

1

WHAT DOES BEING CATHOLIC MEAN?

Catholics trace their beliefs to Jesus' last three years of life and the teachings and practices of the Twelve Apostles. No study of Catholicism would be complete without an understanding of the word *Catholic*. The word itself comes from the Greek *katholikos*, meaning "general" or "universal," which appeared in Greek writings before the rise of Christianity.

Writing in A.D. 110, St. Ignatius of Antioch was one of the first to use the phrase *katholike ekklesia* (literally, "catholic church"), but the force behind the phrase's meaning came from St. Cyril of Jerusalem in A.D. 386: "The Church is called Catholic because it extends through all the world and because it teaches universally and without omission all the doctrines which ought to come to human knowledge."

It is clear from the New Testament, particularly Matthew 24:14, that Christ intended His Word to extend beyond Jewish Palestine to all nations. By the end of the first century A.D., at least 100 communities of "Christians" were established in and around the Mediterranean.

Since then, the Word has spread farther still, to nearly one billion people, across state lines and over cultural boundaries. What's more, these various cultures have adapted Catholic rites and created variations that the Church accepts fully at some times and reluctantly at others.

Tradition is key to understanding Catholicism. According to Catholic thought, the Bible is considered to be a product of traditions, pulled together from numerous sources and over a long period of time.

Catholics form diverse communities of varied ethnic and national groups that share a sense of belonging to the formal institution of the Catholic Church. The Second Vatican Council defined the Church as "a kind of sacrament or sign of intimate union with God, and of the unity of all mankind." In joining the Church, each member joins an institution that comprises the Body of Christ on Earth.

The local congregation, ministered to by a priest, is the basic unit of Catholic community. Each congregation is part of a larger diocese (the territory under a bishop's jurisdiction), and all the dioceses in the world answer to the Curia in Rome. In combination, these units make up one living, breathing entity that prays and worships in the same way, forming a huge community of souls.

A specific belief in and understanding of God is at the heart of the religious aspect of Catholicism. Catholics learn how to live their lives based on their devotion to God, and Catholicism offers a way of life that is based on particular doctrines, faith, theology, and a firm sense of moral responsibility. These elements, based on the Scriptures or "divine revelations," later evolved through tradition. Other religions may contain some or many of these elements, but these specific liturgical, ethical, and spiritual orientations give Catholicism its distinctive character.

In practical terms, being Catholic also means sharing a sense of community and mutual responsibility that is reinforced through thousands of service organizations that the Church sponsors around the world. Service to others is elemental to Catholicism. Out of love for the Lord, the

Church is expected to serve humankind compassionately, both through its service institutions and through the work of individual Catholics.

∽∾ 2 ∽∾

CATHOLICISM COMPARED TO OTHER CHRISTIAN COMMUNITIES

Christians have many ways of practicing their faith—through the Catholic Church, the Eastern Orthodox Church, and the many Protestant denominations, among which are the Baptists, Lutherans, Methodists, and Presbyterians. All Christians share their belief in and acceptance of Jesus Christ, but they also differ in many important ways.

In the Great Schism of 1054, the Church underwent its first split into the Eastern and Western Churches. (For more information on the Great Schism, see Number 15.) Then, much later, in the sixteenth and seventeenth centuries, the Protestant movements split the Western Church further into the Roman Catholic and Protestant denominations.

The word *Protestant* is derived from "protest": The Protestant faiths splintered from the Catholic Church because ordinary people protested against the Catholic institution and some of its conduct and practices, particularly the view that the Church is necessary for salvation.

Interestingly, although the head of the Catholic Church has been situated in Rome for many centuries, the word *Roman* was not appended to the Catholic Church until the Reformation. The followers of Martin

Luther, the group that made the first major split from the Church, also considered themselves Catholic. They described the Church as "Roman" to indicate the distinction between themselves and followers of "Romish" or "Papist" Catholics.

In some ways, the Protestant churches are similar to the Catholic Church. Most believe in the importance of the Bible, the Resurrection of Jesus Christ, the Triune God (Father, Son, and Holy Ghost), and other Christian doctrines and practices. Unlike the Catholic Church, Protestant churches recognize only Baptism and the Eucharist as sacraments. (In the Protestant faiths, other significant events, such as marriage and the ordination of ministers, are considered rituals rather than sacraments.)

The main distinction between Catholicism and Protestantism is that Catholicism is a religion of sacraments (seeing the spiritual enfleshed in the secular world) while Protestantism is more a religion of the bodiless Word of God. Sacramentality is rooted in the idea that everything reveals God. Over time, Protestantism has retained only parts of this concept. Protestants don't believe, as Catholics do, in the special significance of Mary. They also don't believe in transubstantiation (that the Eucharist is, after the declaration by a priest, the Body and Blood of Christ). They believe that priests and ministers are merely members of the laity, trained in the practices of a particular religion, rather than actual mediators of God's grace. Finally, Protestants see religious statues and icons more as forms of idolatry than as windows to the spiritual world, as Catholics do.

Another significant difference lies in the Catholic and Protestant approaches to the Bible. Catholics believe that the Church—as the authentic moral and theological authority—should be their guide in interpreting the Bible. Protestants challenge this view. Many Protestant communities accept personal interpretation of the Bible as they do a personal (unmediated) relationship between each person and God.

In Catholic ideology, the pope, as head of the Church hierarchy, is infallible in matters of faith and morals, because he is the representative of Christ on Earth. This belief is known as the Petrine Primacy or apostolic succession, because the pope follows a line of succession back to St. Peter, the first bishop of the early Church, who received his appointment directly from Jesus. However, many Protestants deny that the pope is infallible in such matters and reject the doctrine of apostolic succession.

There is also a difference in how Protestants and Catholics worship. Until recently, Catholics celebrated the Mass with a highly structured, formal ceremony conducted in Latin. (Today, most Catholic churches in the United States and many other countries have made a switch to having services in the vernacular—the language of the people.) Protestant forms of worship are simpler: Believers pray in their native tongues and there is more preaching. In some denominations, the service is completely unstructured, allowing the congregation a much greater degree of participation.

Part 1

HISTORY

UNDERSTANDING CATHOLICISM MEANS NOT ONLY GAINING a grasp of the Catholic belief system, but also examining the Church's place in world history and modern Western society. For almost two millennia, the Church's impact has been profound. In its early days, there were many interpretations of Christianity. Over a period of three or four centuries, however, the Catholic version gained ascendancy.

The Church traces its origins to Jesus and then to the ministry of His Apostles. From there, in the early centuries after Christ's death, the first "popes" carried on those earliest traditions and developed the organizational structure, doctrines, dogmas, and devotions that have become integral parts of the faith.

Through the centuries, the Church as an institution became a dominant force. Popes and other clergy influenced nations and politics, and politics, in turn, had an impact on the Church. Although many strides in the development of the faith were made, the Church also abused its powers and dominance at times.

In recent centuries, the Catholic Church has struggled with the sweeping social changes wrought by the Enlightenment, the Industrial Revolution, the rise of democracy, and a move toward individualism—developments that have, for good or ill, sometimes run counter to Catholic ideology. Over the past forty years (since the Second Vatican Council, 1962–1965), the Church has, to its credit, looked at itself honestly, apologized for past transgressions, and worked to adjust to the concerns of modern times.

The Annunciation and the birth of Jesus

The story of the Catholic Church and the root of its belief system must begin with Jesus Christ and His human life. Catholic doctrine teaches that Jesus had a dual nature: He was both human and divine. Jesus the Son of God was made a man as a perfect expression of God's love.

When it comes to documenting Jesus' life as a historical human being, Catholic scholars and laypeople rely on the main written source, the Bible, but books by early Roman historians also mention His existence. The most important of these sources is *Jewish Antiquities,* a historical work written by Flavius Josephus, one of the world's earliest historians.

Flavius Josephus was born in Jerusalem in A.D. 37 to a priestly Jewish family. Although he was involved in the First Revolt against Rome, he later switched sides and moved to Rome, where he wrote his historical accounts under the auspices of the Roman emperor. The *Jewish Antiquities* is a collection of twenty books that discuss the history of the Jewish people. While the original text no longer exists, the earliest existing versions of the manuscript include the following reference:

> Now, there was about this time Jesus, a wise man, if it be lawful to call him a man, for he was a doer of wonderful works— a teacher of such men as receive the truth with pleasure. He drew over to him both many of the Jews, and many of the Gentiles. He was [the] Christ.

According to the Bible, Jesus Christ was born to the daughter of Anne and Joachim, Mary, who was chosen by God to bear His Son. A rare and important reference to Mary in the New Testament concerns her visit from the Angel Gabriel. He appeared to her and announced: "You will conceive in your womb and bear a son" (Luke 1:31; Luke 1:26–38 tells the story of the Annunciation).

At the time, Mary was betrothed to the carpenter Joseph, and the social stigma of bearing a child outside of wedlock was enormous. Indeed, Joseph intended to quietly divorce her. But an angel also appeared to Joseph to explain that he would be head of a household in which Mary would bear the coming Messiah. And so Joseph too accepted his role, as Jesus' earthly father.

Although Mary and Joseph lived in Nazareth, and Jesus is often known as Jesus of Nazareth, He was actually born in Bethlehem. According to the Gospel of Luke, Mary and Joseph had to travel to Bethlehem for the census. The town was full of people and the only place where the couple could find a place to sleep was in a manger. It was there that Jesus was born, and also where He was visited by the three wise men, the Magi (as depicted in familiar Nativity scenes every Christmastime).

When Herod heard from the Magi that the King of the Jews was born, he sent out soldiers to kill all Jewish boys two years old and younger. To save their son, Joseph and Mary fled to Egypt. Only after Herod died did the family return to their home in Nazareth.

4

JESUS' LIFE AND MINISTRY

When studying the origins of Catholicism, it is important to keep in mind that Jesus of Nazareth was Jewish. He was born into a Jewish family and raised in the Jewish tradition; consequently, Jewish heritage and belief played an integral role in Jesus' teaching and ministry.

Little is mentioned in the New Testament regarding Jesus' early childhood years, until He reached the age of twelve. At that point, His parents found Him in the temple conversing with the elders, demonstrating that even at a young age, Jesus was a person of strong conviction and an eloquent, passionate speaker.

According to the Bible, Jesus' formal ministry began with John the Baptist (his cousin, the son of Elizabeth and Zachariah). Also known as the Precursor, John baptized Jesus in the River Jordan. Jesus' baptism was a highly symbolic undertaking in which His message of love was expressed in the triune acts of repentance, forgiveness, and the washing away of sins.

Immediately after His baptism, Jesus retired to the desert of Judea for a forty-day fast. Here, according to the Gospel of Mark and the Gospel of Luke, Satan subjected Him to three assaults, or temptations:

1. That to relieve His hunger, He change the rocks to bread
2. That He cast Himself off a parapet to see if the angels would catch Him
3. That in exchange for worship, He receive dominion over all the kingdoms of the Earth

Jesus' time in the desert is considered a preparation for His ministry. In His ministering, Jesus traveled for three years around Galilee. A small province of ancient Palestine, Galilee was part of the Roman Empire. According to the Gospels, Jesus also preached in and around Jerusalem.

Jesus' preaching alarmed the local authorities almost immediately—first the Pharisees (those who practiced strict adherence to Jewish religious laws) and then the Romans. When some people began to proclaim

Jesus as the King of the Jews, both the Jewish religious leaders and the Roman government began to see Him as a threat.

∞ 5 ∞

THE APOSTLES AND THE GOSPEL WRITERS

Jesus had many disciples and devoted followers during His lifetime. From them, He picked twelve men to travel with Him. After Jesus' death, these disciples came to be known as the Apostles, from the Greek word *apostolos*, "to send forth." Jesus taught them, so that they would one day go out into the world to spread His message. The Twelve Apostles were:

- Peter and his brother Andrew
- James the Greater and John, also brothers. (This John is not to be confused with John the Baptist, who had a separate role as the Precursor—the one who announced that the Son of God was coming.)
- Philip, Bartholomew, Matthew, Thomas, James (son of Alphaeus), Thaddaeus (son of James), and Simon
- Judas Iscariot, who would betray Jesus for thirty pieces of silver

Later, Paul would join the Christians and come to be regarded by the eleven original Apostles as their peer. Thus, Paul became a sort of "honorary" Apostle because of the power and influence of his teaching and preaching, particularly to the Gentiles.

It was the disciples' special privilege to stay close to Jesus and receive His training and wisdom. As witnesses to Jesus' life on Earth and students of His teachings, the disciples who became the Apostles also became founders of the Church and the sources of the Gospels (first passed down orally and eventually written down). The Gospels, apostolic letters, and other writings were later compiled into the New Testament.

Jesus chose Peter, a married fisherman who lived in Galilee, to be the leader of the disciples, and eventually the new Church. Peter's name was originally Simon; later, Jesus came to call him Cephas ("rock," in Aramaic). Later still, this name came into Greek as Peter (*petros* being Greek for "rock"). The new name denoted Peter's central function in Jesus' inner circle: "And so I say to you, you are Peter, and upon this rock I will build my church" (Matthew 16:18). Jesus' choice of a fisherman and the name He gave him are both symbolic. Jesus chose Peter to be a fisher of men, the first in the apostolic line of those who would later follow him.

Two of the Gospels in the New Testament were attributed to the Apostles Matthew and John. (The other two were attributed to Mark and Luke.) The word *gospel* means "good news," and the four Gospels of the New Testament present the news of Jesus Christ's life and teachings. Each Gospel had a different message and concentrated on different aspects of interpreting the life, teaching, and meaning of Jesus.

Although not one of the original Apostles, Mark was probably a disciple of Jesus. The Gospel of Mark focuses on Jesus' suffering, which persecuted Christians could identify with. Most likely written in Rome, somewhere around A.D. 65–70, Mark's is said to be the clearest and the shortest of the four Gospels, and it contains more miracle stories and fewer teachings than the others. Mark also tells readers how patterning their lives after Jesus', especially His self-sacrificing love, is what it means to be a Christian, and that this is where hope lies.

Matthew, a tax collector before he left that work at Jesus' directive, probably wrote his Gospel in Hebrew. (It is believed that a well-educated Grecian Jew later translated it into Greek.) Matthew's gospel explains how Jesus, as the Messiah, fulfills Jewish prophecies. He also emphasized Christians growing together in faith, in a community of love.

A companion of St. Paul's, Luke was a physician from Antioch (some say Greece) who never actually met Jesus. It is likely that he wrote the Third Gospel in Greece around the year A.D. 85. Luke's gospel was directed at Christians who had been pagans. His work is marked by its concern for those who needed good words the most and were most often left out: women, the poor, and so on. It points out how Jesus, as Savior, does not discriminate on the basis of race, class, or gender. It is Luke who gives an account of the Nativity, stressing how humble Jesus' birth was.

John was one of Jesus' Twelve Apostles. Born in Galilee, he was the brother of James the Greater, another Apostle. John was a fisherman until Jesus called him. One of the three Apostles closest to Jesus (the others were James the Greater and Peter), John was, along with Peter, the first Apostle at the tomb after the Resurrection. John was the only Apostle at the Crucifixion, and it was there that Jesus placed His mother, Mary, into

John's care. The Gospel of John, written circa A.D. 90 (some say circa A.D. 110), formulates the difficult notion of Jesus as a divine being, although it also stresses Jesus' humanity. The author of the Gospel of John was almost certainly *not* a disciple of Jesus. He was, more likely, a follower or acquaintance of John. The Gospel of John takes a more philosophical and theological approach than the other Gospels. It is a Gospel that was likely written after a period of long reflection, unlike the other Gospels, which serve more as documentation of events.

6

THE TEN COMMANDMENTS

The Ten Commandments are also known as the Decalogue. Drawn from the Hebrew Bible, they have great significance in the Catholic Church. The first three commandments are those God gave for appropriate worship of Him. The next seven attest to behavior toward neighbors. The basic obligations of religion and morality are as follows.

1. I am the Lord your God. You shall not have strange gods before me.
2. You shall not take the name of the Lord in vain. [Oaths, perjury, and blasphemy are forbidden.]
3. Keep the Sabbath holy. [The Church interprets this commandment to mean that attendance at Mass on Sunday is expected,

and that on this day a good Catholic should not turn his or her mind to other distractions, like work. The Sabbath is a day of worship.]

4. Honor your father and your mother.
5. You shall not kill.
6. You shall not commit adultery.
7. You shall not steal.
8. You shall not bear false witness against your neighbor.
9. You shall not covet your neighbor's wife.
10. You shall not covet your neighbor's goods.

The Catholic Church teaches that sinful humanity needed the revelation of these commandments to help them live a moral life and, by proper observance to achieve a state of grace. The Catechism of the Catholic Church states that the commandments "express man's fundamental duties."

When, in order to test Him, the Pharisees questioned Jesus regarding which is the greatest commandment in the Law, Jesus replied:

Love the Lord your God with all your heart and with all your soul and with all your mind. This is the first and greatest commandment. And the second is like it: Love your neighbor as yourself. All the Law and the Prophets hang on these two commandments (Matthew 22:36–40).

In this way, Jesus summed up the spirit of all of the Commandments.

THE BEATITUDES: ACHIEVING SUPREME HAPPINESS

Although those in power felt threatened by Jesus' work and teaching, it's important to note that He was not preaching a new religion. He brought people a message that came to be regarded as the Word of God, and He taught that every person can receive salvation. As a Jew addressing other Jews, He reminded people that following the letter of the law (literal observance of religious laws, ceremonies, and practices) was not as important as following the spirit of the law (the true, spiritual meaning and intention behind laws) and living a good life on Earth.

Jesus taught His message of love with clarity and simplicity. He taught God's infinite love for the humble and the weak, and He taught that each person should strive to follow God's will.

During the Sermon on the Mount, Jesus addressed His largest audience in the hills of the Galilee, where He gave His followers a series of blessings, known as the Beatitudes (Matthew 5:3–11):

Blessed are the poor in spirit, for theirs is the kingdom of Heaven.
Blessed are they who mourn, for they will be comforted.
Blessed are the meek, for they will inherit the land.
Blessed are they who hunger and thirst for righteousness,
   for they will be satisfied.

Blessed are the merciful, for they will be shown mercy.

Blessed are the clean of heart, for they will see God.

Blessed are the peacemakers, for they will be called children of God.

Blessed are they who are persecuted for the sake of righteousness,
for theirs is the kingdom of Heaven.

Blessed are you when they insult you and persecute you and utter
every kind of evil against you [falsely] because of me.

The word *beatitude* actually means "supreme happiness." It is not always easy to be happy in this imperfect, earthly existence. (Achieving true happiness can be particularly difficult in these modern, materialistic times, when everyday life is so stressful.) But Jesus wanted His followers to achieve happiness, so He gave them the beatitudes as guidelines.

The beatitudes portray Jesus' charity. Beautiful and paradoxical, they are precepts meant to comfort believers and inspire them to practice that same charity. Time and again, Jesus Christ stressed compassion for the meek, the poor, the oppressed, the hungry, and the disenfranchised. Jesus spoke eloquently of such individuals during His Sermon on the Mount, and He certainly identified with those who were downtrodden by the powerful or corrupt. Catholics, in turn, recognize that they should follow Jesus' example and also help the poor and hungry, work for human rights, support peaceful action for freedom in countries where people are not allowed to worship as they wish, and stress the right of all people to live in peace and harmony.

8

GRAPPLING WITH JESUS' DEATH

Central to the Catholic faith is the paschal mystery of Christ's death and Resurrection. Jesus had to suffer and die so that humankind could be saved.

Jesus' brief life—thirty-three years in total—culminated in Jerusalem. The last events of His life, from the Last Supper to His crucifixion, are known collectively as the Passion.

The Passion begins with the Last Supper, a Passover meal that Jesus ate with His disciples. Catholics and many Protestant denominations celebrate this important ceremony, now known as the Eucharist. Such Christians believe that Jesus invited His followers to enjoy communion with Him forever by literally partaking of His Body and Blood through consecrated bread and wine. The Eucharist is the heart of the Catholic Mass.

After the Last Supper, the Disciples left Jesus in the Garden of Gethsemane, where He prayed. There, after being betrayed by His own disciple, Judas, soldiers found Jesus and arrested Him. Jesus was tried and taken to Golgotha with two criminals, and the three were crucified.

According to Church teachings, the Crucifixion is also known as the Agony: Jesus died on the cross to atone for our sins. It is also considered a sacrifice: God sacrificed His Son for us.

The earthly cause of Jesus' death is attributed to the enmity of some religious Jews (who thought that Jesus was acting against the law and the temple) and the Roman rulers in Palestine (who feared insubordination and rebellion among the Jews and wished to make the death of the so-called King of the Jews an example).

Pharisees accused Jesus of demonic possession, blasphemy, and false prophecy—although Jesus made it clear that He came not "to abolish the law or the prophets . . . but to fulfill. . . . Whoever breaks one of the least of these commandments and teaches others to do so will be called least in the kingdom of Heaven" (Matthew 5:16–18). Jesus also showed respect for the temple, the dwelling of His Father, a holy place. He was angered that it had become a bargain warehouse, and He drove out the moneychangers. "My house shall be a house of prayer, but you are making it a den of thieves" (Matthew, 21:13).

But there was another reason that events unfolded as they did. The Church teaches that Jesus' death was part of God's plan, long foretold by the Scriptures, especially by the prophet Isaiah, who referred to Him as the suffering servant (Isaiah 53:7–8). Jesus took on humankind's sin and the suffering attached to it. As the sacrificial Paschal Lamb, He offered His life to the Father for our sins, out of pure love for us. His death was the sacrifice of the New Covenant, which helped restore people to communion with God.

As such, the Church does not hold any specific individuals, groups, or races responsible for the death of Christ. The Church teaches that all sinners are responsible for Christ's death: "We must regard as guilty all those who continue to relapse into their sins. Since our sins made the Lord Christ suffer the torment of the cross, those who plunge themselves into disorders and crimes crucify the Son of God anew in their hearts" (Roman Catechism I, 5, 11).

THE RESURRECTION AND THE ASCENSION: FULFILLMENT OF OLD TESTAMENT PROPHESIES

After He died, Jesus' mother and other followers laid His body in a tomb cut in the rock and sealed with a large stone. Three days after His death, Mary Magdalene—another follower of Christ—discovered that the tomb was empty. Jesus had been resurrected. According to the Gospels, Mary met Jesus on the road, and, later, He appeared to and communed with His disciples, and then ascended into Heaven.

The physical resurrection of Jesus Christ is a crucial event in Christianity that is fundamental to Catholic belief. This most important of all Jesus' miracles is what Catholics celebrate every Easter. It is a symbol of renewal, and it brings us the message that even though we are all sinners, we can be reborn in Christ, our Savior.

The Resurrection fulfilled the promises of the Old Testament and those made by Jesus during His life, and it confirmed His divinity. Jesus had said, "When you lift up the Son of Man, then you will realize that I AM" (John 8:28).

The Church holds that the Resurrection is important for another reason as well. By suffering and dying, Jesus redeemed human beings from sin. The Church teaches that by rising, He opened the way to new life. This new life justified human beings. It gave them victory over death, which is caused by sin, and allowed them to be filled with grace.

Following His Resurrection, Jesus spent forty days and forty nights with His Disciples, living with the appearance of an ordinary man. Then, He ascended into Heaven, rising up body and soul. This occurrence is known as the Ascension, and it has great significance for Catholics. It reaffirms that Jesus came from the Father and has returned to Him. Through Christ, mankind now has access to the Father's house, by growing close to Christ and following Him. The Church teaches that Jesus is in the presence of God on our behalf, exercising His priesthood in order to intercede for those who follow Him.

The Church holds that, as Jesus sits at the right hand of God, and as one with God, He shows forth His power and might. He exercises His dominion over the Kingdom of God, a "kingdom that will have no end," "the kingdom of Christ is already present in mystery," "on earth, the seed and the beginning of the kingdom" (Nicene Creed). However, the final fulfillment will come when Jesus returns to Earth, which is why Catholics pray for the Second Coming of Christ. Meanwhile, humankind must endure the trials of physical and moral evil with the guidance of the Spirit.

∽ 10 ∾

PENTECOST: THE BIRTHDAY OF THE CATHOLIC CHURCH

The Catholic Church formally considers its beginning to be the first Pentecost after Jesus' crucifixion. But what, exactly, is meant by "Pentecost"?

A few weeks after the Ascension of Christ, the disciples had gathered in Jerusalem with Mary, the Mother of God, to observe *Shavuot*, the Feast of Weeks—a Jewish holiday held fifty days after the Passover Sabbath to celebrate the midseason grain harvest. (Pentecost, "the fiftieth day," is a Greek translation of the Hebrew *Shavuot*.)

This particular occasion probably wasn't much of a celebration, however. Jesus' disciples were confused and unsure of what to do next. They probably grieved their teacher, and it's likely that they were anxious about their personal safety. Yet, it is reported that what they experienced during this feast day transformed them:

> And suddenly there came from the sky a noise like a strong driving wind, and it filled the entire house in which they were. Then there appeared to them tongues as of fire, which parted and came to rest on each one of them. And they were all filled with the Holy Spirit and began to speak in different tongues, as the Spirit enabled them (Acts 2:2–4).

The Disciples were filled with the Holy Spirit, which cemented their belief and gave them courage and the gift of tongues. This gave the Disciples the ability to speak so that people of different languages could comprehend their meaning. They went out, and they began to preach. At this point, the disciples became Apostles.

It is taught that Peter, filled with the Holy Spirit, preached with such joy that 3,000 were baptized that very day. These converts were Jews from

Mesopotamia, Judea, Cappadocia, and many other places. Visiting Jerusalem for the holiday, they took Peter's message with them back to their homes. Peter's central role in the expanding circle of Christ's followers was thus clearly defined, and the Church was made public.

The Apostles proceeded to spread the word in and around the Mediterranean region, drawing in people from all races and religions, and establishing Christian communities wherever they went. This was their mission, and it came with great tests of faith. Sometimes they were welcomed. At other times, they placed themselves in great personal peril—and, ultimately, some were martyred for their faith.

Today, the Church celebrates Pentecost, the day when the Holy Spirit descended to the disciples, fifty days after Easter Sunday. Originally, the Feast of the Ascension of Christ was also celebrated during Pentecost, but by the late fourth century A.D. its date had been moved back ten days, and the Ascension is now celebrated forty days after Easter.

∞ 11 ∞

LEADERSHIP IN THE EARLY DAYS OF THE CHURCH

Christianity shifted its center from Jerusalem to Rome around A.D. 70, when the Romans suppressed a Jewish rebellion and destroyed Jerusalem. Peter, proclaimed by Jesus to be the rock of the Church, worked and died in Rome, as did Paul. In the Church's view, Peter left behind a line of apostolic succession of bishops (or popes) who would maintain the Roman bishopric—the diocese of the bishop—as the spiritual center of the Catholic Church.

As the Church continued to grow, a number of strong, forceful characters helped to shape its development. The Church would not be what it is today without the work and thought of these important people.

Clement of Rome became the third Bishop of Rome around the end of the first century A.D. Some evidence—though no proof—suggests that he worshiped with Peter and Paul. If so, he was quite close to the source of divine inspiration, and its influence on him would have been great.

Clement's fame comes mainly from one masterful letter in which he asserts the inviolable authority and primacy of the Church of Rome, which descends from Peter through apostolic succession. Clement wrote his letter to the church of the Corinthians, who had been led into sedition, and he demanded their return to obedience.

Clement may have suffered a martyr's death. According to a story from the fourth century A.D., Emperor Trajan was upset that Clement had converted so many pagans to Christianity and banished him to a quarry, where he performed a miracle and slaked the thirst of thousands. Trajan then ordered Clement to be weighted down with an iron anchor and tossed into the sea near Crimea. When the waves subsided, legend has it Clement was entombed in marble by angels.

Ignatius of Antioch, the third bishop of Antioch, lived from the first to second centuries A.D. He was a good pastor and gave his people courage when the Emperor Domitian began persecuting Christians.

Ignatius was a strong and impassioned writer. He sent epistles to various churches—to the Ephesians, Magnesians, Trallians, Romans, Philadelphians, Smyrnaeans, and to the great bishop Polycarp, a founding father of the Church. In his letters, Ignatius warned against heresies. A heresy is a challenge to an integral, accepted Church belief. For example, two views that weren't considered heresies until the fourth century A.D. were Arianism, which denied Jesus' divinity, and Manichaeism, which taught that one god created good and another created evil, and that mortals were not responsible for their sins. Ignatius's letters explained that heresies were a threat to Church unity.

Before the Council of Nicaea in A.D. 325, there existed multiple interpretations of what it meant to be Christian. Because up to that point no one had crystallized essential Christian teachings, there was no consistent orthodox standard of beliefs against which to judge other divergent beliefs as "heresies." At the time of the Council of Nicaea, however, the Church began to assert core teachings, such as Jesus' divinity. This belief would not reach its final formalization until A.D. 381, at the Council of Constantinople. From the time of the Council of Nicaea until the Council of Constantinople, the acceptance of this teaching remained a serious source of conflict and contention within the early Church.

Ignatius of Antioch continued to write while under arrest and on his way to Rome. He was sentenced to be torn apart by lions at the Flavian amphitheater in Rome, and he died a martyr.

Irenaeus of Lyon grew up in Smyrna, where he remembered hearing Bishop Polycarp talk about the Apostle John. Irenaeus was ordained in Lyon.

There, he witnessed the horrifying martyrdom of Greek-speaking Christians, including Lyon's bishop. Irenaeus traveled to Rome to tell the bishop, who asked Irenaeus to return to Lyon, take over the duties of the martyred bishop of Lyon, and help rebuild the Christian Church. (By "Church," the pope meant the Christian community, not a physical building.)

In his writings, Irenaeus argued against the Gnostics, who did not accept the humanity of Jesus Christ because they saw the body as evil. Irenaeus also fought for and helped perpetuate the idea of apostolic succession.

Clement of Alexandria was a second-century teacher who traveled among the Greek-speaking Christian communities before settling in Alexandria to start a school. He is known for three important philosophical works expressing his ideas: *The Protrepticus, The Paedogogus* ("The Tutor"), and *The Stromateis*. One of his ardent beliefs was that a Christian life should be devoted to the perfect knowledge of truth.

∽ 12 ∾

CHRISTIANITY SPREADS TO ROME

For its first 300 years, Christianity was viewed with great suspicion. Christian communities grew, but people often joined them at great personal peril. Believers usually worshiped in secret. Christians were harassed and persecuted throughout the Roman Empire; they had no political power.

The empire itself was under stress from without and within. Roman territories were under barbarian attack, while at home the Roman aristocracy was growing weak and corrupt. Under siege and without great leaders, Rome was disintegrating.

In A.D. 312, the Roman army stationed in Britain elected Constantine the next Roman emperor. He returned to Rome, knowing that he would have to fight for his position when he got there. As Constantine rode through France with his army, he had a vision of a cross. He took this as a sign and ordered his soldiers to paint the Greek letters for the word *Christ* on their shields. Constantine defeated his rival and entered Rome victorious, as the new emperor. Although he did not convert to Christianity until shortly before his death many years later, both he and Rome officially supported Christianity.

As the author of the Edict of Milan, which allowed Christians the freedom to worship openly and freely, Constantine is an extremely important figure in Church history. He also moved the capital of the Roman Empire east to Byzantium (modern-day Istanbul), and renamed it Constantinople. This new "Rome" gave Christianity a fresh start. Moreover, in A.D. 325 Constantine summoned the Council of Nicaea, a congregation of 300 bishops who formalized some of the doctrines of Christian faith. (See Number 81.) This marks a substantial turning point in history, because from that point, the Roman state became formally involved in Church affairs.

Theodosius the Great, a military leader who lived from A.D. 346 to 395, was baptized in 380 after he became sick and nearly died. The last emperor to rule both the eastern and western Roman empires, Theodosius tolerated pagan practices early in his reign. Toward the end of his life, he became stricter, slowly eroding pagan power and rights to worship, until he outlawed pagan practices altogether.

Theodosius streamlined Church unity by suppressing the Arian and Manichean heresies in Constantinople. He is also known for calling the second General Council of Constantinople, in A.D. 381, to provide for a Catholic succession in the patriarchal see of Constantinople (the group of five "superior" bishops in the Eastern Orthodox Church hierarchy).

∽ 13 ∽

THE INFLUENCE OF THE PAPACY GROWS

In the fourth century A.D., the power of the bishop in Rome continued to grow. Pope Damasus I (A.D. 366–384) and each of those who followed him—Siricius, Anastasius I, Innocent I, Zosimus, Boniface I, Celestine I, Sixtus III, and Pope Leo the Great—made the Church more powerful and established the idea that when they spoke a papal utterance, Peter was speaking through them. After Rome fell in A.D. 410, during the papacy of Innocent I, the pope moved to fill the vacuum in political leadership.

Subsequently, popes often wrote about the glory of the Church in Rome, and from this, the formal title Holy Roman Catholic Church arose. "The entire Catholic Church spread over the globe is the sole bridal chamber of Christ," wrote the influential Pope Damasus. (Remember, *catholic* means "universal" or "all-embracing.") "The Church of Rome has been placed above all other churches not by virtue of conciliar decree, but by virtue of the words of the Lord: 'Thou art Peter!'" This was a very controversial view, clearly not accepted by other bishops.

Pope Leo the Great, who held the papal office from A.D. 440 to 461, was a man of enormous personal strength and of great eloquence: He persuaded Attila the Hun to turn from the gates of Rome when the barbarians planned to sack the city. Leo's most significant achievement was forcefully asserting the primacy of the Roman bishop's position. He coaxed Emperor Valentinian to recognize the status of this role officially. As a result, in A.D. 445, Valentinian issued an edict proclaiming the papal supremacy of the Bishop of Rome, for all time.

In A.D. 451, Pope Leo greatly influenced the Council of Chalcedon, where doctrine on Jesus' dual nature was firmly established. (That Jesus the Christ was both fully human and fully divine is a critical Catholic doctrine.) The Council also affirmed that the Bishop of Rome had higher authority than the patriarch of Constantinople. This proclamation festered over five centuries of bickering and led to the eventual schism between the Eastern Orthodox and the Roman Catholic (Western) Church.

Over time, the Church became increasingly involved in secular (and especially political) affairs. Three men—Gregory, Boniface (a monk), and Gregory VII—were especially instrumental in shaping the papal office. Pope Gregory I, who was born in about A.D. 540, started his career as a civil servant in Rome trying to feed the poor. He gave up his job and established a monastery, living a quiet life. When the pope died of the plague, the people elected Gregory to the office, at the age of fifty.

He accomplished many things during his tenure, demonstrating what could be achieved in both the world at large and in the spiritual world. He tried to look after the poor, he helped rebuild the aging churches, he mandated education for priests, he spread the faith to Britain, and he wrote extensively on matters of theology. He also created the beautiful liturgical music known as Gregorian chant.

Boniface, an English Benedictine monk, is another individual who contributed to the Western Church's centralization of power. His great mission was to preach to the Germanic states, for which he was made a bishop. He established monasteries and earned the trust of German (then called Frankish) rulers.

In A.D. 751, with the approval of the pope, Boniface crowned Pepin the Short as king of the French. This relationship between the papacy and the French monarchy let the pope appeal to the Franks for help when a barbarian tribe threatened Rome. Pepin defended Rome and then gave the pope a huge area of land in Italy as his own territory. This move proved to be extremely significant, as it meant that the pope was now a territorial, as well as a spiritual, ruler: The Papal States were born, and an arrangement of popes crowning kings and kings helping popes took shape.

With the establishment of the Papal States, the Church not only had a home, but a country, of its own. The papacy continued to claim ownership of vast land holdings until 1870. Today, Vatican City is what remains as a separate state.

14

MONASTICISM

While the bishops—and the Bishop of Rome, in particular—were getting more involved in worldly affairs, some believers wanted to distance themselves from secular life and wholly devote themselves to God. Thus, the fourth century A.D. also saw the rise of monasticism, a movement pioneered by hermits who wished to emulate Jesus' sojourn in the wilderness. These hermits sought to lead a quiet, simple life, away from worldly temptations.

T he word *monastery* comes from the Greek word *monos,* meaning "alone" or "single." The first monasteries originated in Egypt, and their monks lived alone and gathered only for prayer in a common chapel. From these early groups of loosely collegial hermits sprang full-fledged communities, with well-defined and centralized systems and doctrines.

St. Augustine (A.D. 354–430), one of the early monks, played an important role in Church theology through his development of a theological tradition. As a young man, Augustine was not pious. However, he later found his faith with the help of Bishop Ambrose, whom he met in Rome. He then returned to North Africa, where he set up a small monastery.

After Rome fell to the Goths in A.D. 410, everyone wondered how God could allow such a horrible thing to happen. In response to this issue, Augustine wrote *The City of God,* his most important work. It is still read today, as it examines how people can hold onto faith during times of great injustice.

Augustine's most renowned work is *The Confessions,* an autobiographical account of his life and how he found his faith. In this deeply philosophical and personal account, he shows how God's grace is available to everyone, even "prodigal sons" who initially live their lives in idleness.

Another very important player in early monastic development was St. Benedict (A.D. 480–547). Sickened by the crimes and sin around him, St. Benedict introduced the ascetic discipline (a tradition of self-denial that included poverty and chastity) to the monastic setting.

The Benedictine order he founded, on a mountaintop halfway between Naples and Rome, eventually established a style of self-sufficient monasteries, which included vineyards, orchards, a church, a library, and sleeping cells. The Benedictine monastery—in essence a complete economic unit—was the model for others for hundreds of years.

By the fifth century, monasteries had been established all over the populated world: through Africa, the dwindling Roman empire, France, Germany, and even Ireland, where St. Patrick worked to convert the Irish to Christianity.

Both the male and female adherents of the monastic life performed important functions. They ministered to the poor and sick, and they welcomed travelers. They also established libraries and some rudimentary education for children.

Basil, the bishop and monk who established an order in Cappadocia, Asia Minor, was the first to stress the importance of scholarly work (in addition to prayer) in monastic life. Until then, most monks were poorly educated and shunned study. Eventually, the scholarly tradition became an important part of monastic life. In fact, monasteries deserve credit for preserving the literature of antiquity, which had to be transcribed by hand. Monks spent hours laboriously copying and painting the most important sacred works into beautifully illuminated manuscripts.

The Middle Ages were terribly hard on poor people, who were vulnerable to rampant diseases and warring feudal factions. During this time, monasteries became oases of peace and order, providing food, clothing, and shelter. Monasteries also kept the flame of Christianity alive during that difficult period of European history.

THE SEPARATION OF THE ROMAN CATHOLIC AND EASTERN ORTHODOX CHURCHES

The separation of the Greek-speaking Eastern Orthodox Church from the Roman Catholic Church began officially with the Great Schism of 1054, but the actual division didn't happen overnight. It came about gradually, as Rome and Constantinople struggled for political power and religious authority.

Tensions often occurred because the two factions of the Church competed to get more converts to accept their way of practicing Christianity as a way of establishing political and cultural alliances. Such was the case with the conversion of the Slavic people of Eastern Europe.

Many Slavic languages are written in the Cyrillic alphabet. The introduction of the Cyrillic alphabet promoted literacy and allowed the Slavs to translate the Bible and other Christian writings into their own languages.

By the end of the first millennium, Serbians, Russians, and Bulgarians worshiped according to the Eastern rites, while Croatians, Czechs, Magyars, Moravians, Poles, and Slovaks joined the Roman Church.

As previously mentioned, Emperor Constantine moved the capital of the Roman Empire from Rome to Constantinople in A.D. 450. When Charlemagne, the king of France, was crowned Emperor of the Holy Roman Empire by Pope Leo III in A.D. 800, there had been no Western emperor for more than 300 years. The Eastern emperor had—in name anyway—been ruler of the West, once the line of Roman emperors collapsed. This appointment signaled that the West was pulling away, and the powers in the East were not happy about it.

Finally, in 1054, the breach between the Eastern and Western churches reached the point of no return. Michael Cerularius, who was Constantinople's patriarch, decided to take a stand. He proclaimed that the two churches could not work together any more.

Pope Leo IX, who did not want to see a schism between the Christians, sent Cardinal Humbert to Constantinople to negotiate as the pope's representative. However, there were many religious and political disagreements to deal with, and the two sides could not come to terms. When Pope Leo passed away, Cardinal Humbert decided to take aggressive action and excommunicated Michael. Michael reacted with condemnation, arguing that the cardinal was not acting with papal authority.

Michael then declared that he was taking control of the Eastern Orthodox Church, but he lacked the effective power to do so.

∽ 16 ∾

STRIFE AND REFORM IN THE CHURCH
AFTER THE EAST-WEST SCHISM

After the Great Schism, the power of the Roman Catholic Church continued to grow in the West. As Europe was moving from a feudal system to unite into states and kingdoms that were ruled by monarchy, the
popes increased their involvement in the politics of surrounding territories, often exerting significant influence through their religious authority.

Pope Gregory VII, also known as Hildebrand, played an important
role in centralizing the power of the Church. In 1073, Gregory decided
to introduce reforms in how bishops and abbots were to be appointed to
their clerical positions. In the past, such appointments were made by high-
ranking laypeople. That meant the Church was subject to local rulers—a
distinctly compromising position.

To introduce the reform, Gregory declared a ruling against "lay investiture," or clerical appointments by secular leaders. Understandably, the
Holy Roman Emperor Henry IV of Germany, who virtually controlled
the Western world, did not agree with this ruling. Unfazed, Gregory
excommunicated Henry from the Church.

To be reinstated, Henry humbled himself before the pope, but the tensions did not cease. Civil war broke out in Germany, and Gregory called for peace in the empire. When Henry refused to cease fighting, Gregory proclaimed Henry to be deposed. Henry responded by setting up an antipope, Clement III, and managed to win the war. He then attacked Italy—unsuccessfully in 1081, and again in 1083. Upon the second foray, he also wooed the Romans with his generosity, and they betrayed Gregory. The pope escaped to Salerno and died a year later.

The conflict continued until Henry V and Pope Calixtus II reached an agreement, known as the Concordat of Worms (1122), that all bishops would thereafter be consecrated by the Church. The emperor had the right to be present at the ordination and to invest secular powers upon the clergy.

This reform, as well as many others introduced by subsequent popes, was complemented by reform in the lower clergy and in Catholic customs and practices. The Church decreed that priests had to attend a Catholic college before they could be ordained, and introduced the practice of priestly celibacy (priests not being able to marry).

Finally, in the thirteenth century, the Church formally established the seven sacraments, as we know them today: Baptism, Confirmation, the Eucharist, Penance, Anointing of the Sick, Matrimony, and Holy Orders. This was a major decision in defining the essence of Roman Catholicism.

The monumental architecture that the wealthy Church championed further solidified the power and influence of the papacy. At the same time, the Church led the way in education. The first universities grew from small schools that had been set up in conjunction with Catholic cathedrals to large organizations offering students great learning and scholarship. Universities in Italy, France, England, and Germany attracted good teachers and ambitious students and taught subjects such as medicine, philosophy, mathematics, logic, law, and theology.

∽ 17 ∾

THE MENDICANT ORDERS

As previously explained, monasticism has a long history within the Catholic Church. First individually and then in groups, men and women congregated apart from society in order to become closer to God. This tradition grew stronger during the Middle Ages, when new religious orders developed, many which still exist.

Mendicant friars belonged to religious orders that also took vows of poverty, like monks. However, these friars did not only relinquish individual proprietorship; they gave up collective proprietorship as well. As a result, these friars relied on their own work and the charity of others to support their orders. Mendicant friars stayed on the move, preaching and begging for alms in order to survive (which is why they also became known as begging friars). The two most important mendicant orders were the Dominicans and the Franciscans.

Also known as Black Friars, because of the black cloaks they wear over their white robes, the Dominicans took their name from Dominic de Guzman, who was born in 1170. Dominic's primary mission was to convert heretics back to the Christian fold. The Dominican order got its start when Dominic persuaded a number of men to help him in his teaching all over Europe. Eventually, however, members of the Dominican order did settle down into communal houses. Among other things, one of this order's great achievements is the fostering of scholarship.

One of the most well known Dominicans is St. Thomas Aquinas (1225–1274), who disobeyed his wealthy family's wishes when he joined the order. Aquinas studied with learned Dominican teachers like Albert the Great and became a great scholar. His most significant accomplishment was applying the philosophical reasoning of Aristotle to the wisdom of the Bible in his *Summa Theologica,* which would eventually, from the Council of Trent on, be used for any official decrees the Church issued.

Like St. Thomas Aquinas, St. Francis of Assisi, founder of the Franciscan order, turned his back on wealth and comfort, but his personal vow of poverty was more severe than most. Known for his deep connection with animals and the natural world around him, Francis also cared for the sick and the lame—even the lepers whom no one would go near. Eventually he attracted many followers who also adopted his simple style of living and good works, and he took them across Europe. One of the people who became a part of St. Francis's cause was a woman named Clare, who started a convent called the Poor Clares for nuns who wished to spend their lives in prayer.

Though the members of mendicant orders were poor, they were rich in spirit, as they sought to follow the example of Jesus Christ.

∽ 18 ∾

TURBULENT TIMES: THE CRUSADES AND THE INQUISITION

As the Church established itself over much of Europe, and as it continued to wrestle for political power through the Middle Ages, its social vision shifted. The Church and its officers were intent on making (and then keeping) Catholicism the pre-eminent religion, taking the Word of God as far as possible.

The Crusades and Inquisition are among the more unfortunate and tumultuous chapters in the Catholic Church's history. Though differing in their ultimate goals, both of these aggressive episodes shared a misguided belief in the use of force to further religious purposes.

The Crusades

The Crusades—wars fought in the name of Christianity during the Middle Ages—served different political, social, and religious purposes. Although historians disagree on the exact number of Crusades (it depends upon a particular historian's definition of what, exactly, constitutes a Crusade), most claim there were at least seven and agree on four of the major Crusades.

Of course, war in the name of religion stands in stark contrast to Jesus' message of love and peace. At that point in history, however, people saw the Crusades as acts of faith and religious duty.

The First Crusade, in the eleventh century, was a reaction to the take-over of Jerusalem by the Turkish Muslims. Safe travel for pilgrims visiting the Christian holy sites was an important issue at this time. Afraid that the Muslims would destroy those sites, and believing that the Holy Land should be liberated in the name of God, Pope Urban II called for a Crusade. Armies of knights were sent to recover the Holy Land. This episode was the first in a series of similar campaigns, which were undertaken throughout the eleventh, twelfth, and thirteenth centuries.

During the course of the four major Crusades, motivations for fighting strayed further and further from original intentions. The knights in the First Crusade did manage to enter Jerusalem, a victory that resulted in a massacre of Muslims and Jews. However, the Christians could not hold Jerusalem for long, despite the reinforcements that arrived during the Second Crusade. The Third Crusade, led by Richard the Lion-Hearted, recovered some land, but the knights were more interested in booty than a divine cause. During the Fourth Crusade, the knights sailed to Constantinople and ransacked it, as Christians fought other Christians.

Ultimately, the Crusades resulted in little except misery for everyone involved. When examining the progression of the four major Crusades, it's not difficult to see that each one was less noble than the one before.

The Inquisition

The Papal Inquisition began in 1232, under the auspices of Pope Gregory IX, as a reaction to the heresies that threatened Church unity. The purpose of the Inquisition was to ferret out heretics and force them to accept Catholic orthodoxy as practiced and taught by the Church.

Conducted mostly in the south of France, northern Italy, and northern Spain, public inquiries were set up town by town. People were encouraged to report heretics, and because the accusers' identities were kept secret, many came forward with names. Heretics who confessed and recanted received a penance (a kind of religious fine), which could be anything from reciting prayers to enduring a flogging. Those who refused to accept the charges against them and "repent" were punished. In the most extreme cases, some were burned at the stake or hanged.

The Papal Inquisition lasted through most of the thirteenth century, and it reappeared in fifteenth-century Spain in its most virulent form.

In Spain, the Inquisition was conducted under the authorization of the Spanish monarch, although with the blessing of the pope—that is, it was a political as well as a religious institution. (All but the Spanish Inquisition was conducted by Church-appointed inquisitors; the Spanish Inquisition was an instrument of the Spanish monarchy.) King Ferdinand and Queen Isabella (the monarchs who funded Columbus's voyages) needed a cause under which they could unify the Spanish people into a powerful nation. They also needed money.

They chose the unifying force of Catholicism to achieve their goals and asked the pope for permission to begin the Inquisition, with the purpose of "purifying" the land. Muslim and Jewish converts to Catholicism, Protestants, nonbelievers, and Christians who did not see eye-to-eye with particular aspects of the Catholic dogma all needed purifying. Conveniently, the state appropriated all possessions that belonged to those heretics who were executed.

A most unfortunate event in Church history, the Spanish Inquisition horrifies, even to this day.

POLITICAL PROBLEMS GIVE RISE TO THE GREAT PAPAL SCHISM

The 1300s were a ghastly time in Europe. The bubonic plague, or Black Death, ravaged the continent and wiped out a third of its population. No one, from peasants to royalty, was safe. The Church was not spared either, and new priests were hastily ordained to replace those who perished while taking care of their parishioners.

Meanwhile, England and France began the Hundred Years' War. Caught up in the struggle, they were not paying much attention to the Church, and the papacy started to lose its power.

At the beginning of the fourteenth century, power over Europe began shifting back to the secular world. King Philip IV of France drew the papacy into battle by levying taxes on the clergy for defense of the realm. Pope Boniface VIII fought him valiantly, but his efforts were unsuccessful. After Boniface's death in 1303, Philip secured the election of a Frenchman, Bertrand de Got, as pope. "Crowned" in Lyons as Clement V, shortly thereafter he took up residence in Avignon, in the south of France.

Although this move was intended to avoid political tension among the Italian city-states, Clement left the papacy vulnerable to the French monarchy. After Clement died, the next pope declared Avignon the permanent seat for the papacy and surrounded himself with church and government officials to do his bidding. Seven French popes would rule from Avignon before the seat returned to Rome.

The papacy's troubles did not end when Pope Gregory XI returned the seat to Rome in 1377. Upon Gregory's death, under pressure from Roman leaders, the College of Cardinals elected an Italian pope, Urban VI, who proved to be weak and undiplomatic. Unhappy with this choice, the French cardinals returned to Avignon and elected a pope of their own, Clement VII. Some countries gave their allegiance to Urban, while others aligned themselves with Clement VII, dividing the papacy and all of Europe. This calamity, which became known as the Great Papal Schism, lasted for thirty years.

It took the efforts of the Holy Roman Emperor Sigismund to end the Church's ignoble behavior. He called the Council of Constance, which settled the Great Schism in 1417. A Roman pope, Martin V, was elected once again.

The Church was united again under one pope, but papal power had been seriously damaged. Peasants and the growing middle class were shocked and appalled. Monarchs grew stronger and more powerful, and the papacy could no longer control them. These changes set the stage for the Renaissance, and also the Reformation, the Protestant movement that threatened to destroy the Catholic Church.

CORRUPTION OF THE CHURCH HIERARCHY
IN THE SIXTEENTH CENTURY

At the dawn of the sixteenth century, the Holy Roman Catholic Church was beset with internal problems. Its hierarchy was corrupt and disorganized. Wealthy families staffed the leadership positions of churches, bishoprics, and the Roman Curia. These members of the clergy bought and sold clerical positions. Bishops controlled huge territories on behalf of the Church, and Church officials bought and sold indulgences.

An indulgence is a partial reduction of the punishment that is still due for sin after confession and absolution. People earn an indulgence through acts of repentance, such as prayer or fasting, so that they will spend less time in purgatory. (Purgatory, a stage in the soul's journey before it reaches Heaven, is a state of purification for those who die in a state of grace. See Number 44.) In the late Middle Ages, clergy took advantage of people's desire to speed the souls of their deceased relatives to Heaven by selling them indulgences, a practice that reformers strongly denounced.

Meanwhile, the local clergy were not properly educated and did not take care of their flocks. They seldom preached, instructed the young, or ministered to the other needs of their parishioners. Worse, they set a bad example. Some had drinking problems, and others kept mistresses.

Religious orders were no better off. War, political strife, and the Black Death had stymied the growth of monasteries. Discipline in monasteries had waned, and members were no longer concerned about social and cultural conditions in the country. Common worship and common meals had given way to the desire for private property.

The Renaissance popes, who were wealthy patrons of the arts and shrewd statesmen, saw the sorry state of affairs, but they were enjoying the status quo too much. The Lateran Council, which concluded in 1517, called for reforms that included adequate training of clergy; however, the pope at the time, Leo X (1475–1521) failed to support them. This corruption, and the need for reform, paved the way for Martin Luther's movement.

∞ 21 ∞

MARTIN LUTHER AND THE REFORMATION

Martin Luther (1483–1546) was the founder of the Reformation movement, which led to the birth of many Protestant communities. A thoughtful, loyal Catholic and scholar, Luther became an Augustinian monk, studied theology, and eventually became a professor at the University of Wittenberg in Germany.

Introspective and depressive, Luther felt he was not worthy of being saved. But in 1513 he had a spiritual insight: Our faith in God's love is what qualifies us for salvation. Good works are secondary. Man is a sinful vessel, saved only because he is cloaked in God's love.

Luther preached his new vision, but he didn't make an impact until he began his campaign against the selling of indulgences, which—for the right price—promised the rich redemption from purgatory. One of Luther's key arguments was that the pope could not possibly have control over souls in purgatory.

In addition to the concept of salvation in faith alone, Luther's other theological principles have remained central to most Protestant denominations:

Scripture alone. The Bible, especially the New Testament, is the only infallible source and rule of faith; each individual should interpret the Scriptures as he or she sees fit. Nothing written after the New Testament by Christian saints and theologians can claim to have the same authority as the Bible.

The universal priesthood of believers. No person needs to depend on a member of the clergy to act as a mediator between him or her and God. Neither the papacy nor the hierarchy of the Church has any more divine authority than does an ordinary Christian.

Preaching of the Word. One of a minister's primary responsibilities is to preach the message of the Scriptures so as to best reach his audience. As a consequence of this thesis, Protestants condensed the liturgy to an exegesis (a critical explanation and analysis) of the Scriptures and communion and began to conduct services in their native tongues (rather than in Latin).

Luther's movement spread rapidly through Europe, where Protestant churches began to come under the protection of the secular government of some territories. Another reformer, John Calvin, built on Luther's credos and sent missionaries throughout Europe to preach and to organize communities. Switzerland, Scotland, parts of France, and the Netherlands all embraced Calvinism. Calvin's teaching upheld the objectively real presence of Jesus in the Eucharist and stressed this sacrament as a way for believers to relate to God. Baptism was the only other sacrament retained by most Protestant traditions. By the time Calvin, Luther, and other reformers had finished preaching, half of all Europe was Protestant.

∽ 22 ∾

RENEWAL AFTER THE REFORMATION

Partly under the pressure of Protestants and partly from leaders within, the Catholic Church began to renew itself. The sixteenth and seventeenth centuries were a time of the birth and rebirth of religious orders; saints and mystics; dedicated popes; and sweeping reforms ushered in by the Council of Trent (1545–1563).

Among religious orders, the new Oratory of Divine Love, founded in Genoa, Italy, in 1475, involved regular devotions and works of mercy for personal spiritual renewal. Composed of both laypeople and the clergy, it included members of the curia (the collective departments and ministries that assist the pope in governing the Church). Important Christian humanists and reformers, including Gian Pietro Carafa (later Paul VI), came from the ranks of this order.

The Capuchin order branched out from the Franciscans as a result of the struggle against the Reformation. The Augustinians and Dominicans both undertook reforms, and the Dominican Antonio Ghislieri became Pius V (1566–1572), bringing a greater degree of integrity to the papal office.

Also during this period, St. Ignatius of Loyola founded the Jesuit order. (A soldier, Ignatius experienced spiritual enlightenment while recovering from his wounds.) Active and practical, the Jesuits worked for propagation and defense of the faith. Members were recruited carefully and received proper training.

There were several other notable men and women who founded or reformed religious orders during this period, which is often identified as the Catholic Reformation.

Philip Neri (1515–1595) founded the Oratorian Priests. Neri was a cheerful, zestful man with deep spiritual qualities. Prominent in Rome during the latter part of the sixteenth century, as confessor of popes and cardinals, he influenced the transformation of the Curia.

Saint Francis de Sales (1567–1622) founded the Salesians and persuaded the people of the Chablais district of France to return to the Catholic faith. His writings are held to be classic guides to the spiritual life.

St. Jane Frances de Chantal (1572–1641), a protégé of Francis de Sales, founded the order of the Sisters of the Visitation.

St. Vincent de Paul (1581–1660) founded the Congregation of the Mission, which did much to improve the French clergy. With Louise de Marillac, he established the Sisters of Charity in 1633. The nuns of this order were not cloistered. Instead, they went out to work among the poor and the sick and were instrumental in founding many hospitals.

Pope Paul III also hastened papal reform by appointing reformers to the College of Cardinals and by finally convening the Council of Trent (1545–1563), which reaffirmed the primacy of the pope and upheld the importance of tradition. It reminded Catholics that salvation requires hope and charity—manifested in good works—as much as it does faith in God's love. Additionally, it rejected Protestant beliefs on the number and nature of the sacraments.

The council strengthened the authority of the bishops and required each bishop to reside in his diocese. It passed regulations on the granting of indulgences and forbade the practices of simony (buying sacred things and offices) and pluralism (holding more than one diocese). Seminary education and clerical dress became mandatory for the diocesan priests, along with the practice of celibacy. The council encouraged the priests as well as the laity to be active in acquiring virtue and to meditate. The Council of Trent concluded under the reformer Pope Pius IV.

The next pope, Pius V (1504–1572), issued new editions of the Index of Forbidden Books, Catechism, the Breviary (the devotional book of priests), and missal. The new missal transformed the Roman Catholic Mass and made it uniform throughout the Church. This was extremely important, because with all the Catholic churches around the world conducting the Mass the same way, the faithful could attend services anywhere and those services would still feel familiar.

∽∾ 23 ∽∾

CATHOLICISM SPREADS TO THE NEW WORLD

The age of maritime voyages and the discovery of new lands ushered in a missionary era. While the Church's battle with Protestantism raged in Europe, the Catholic fold was increasing in the New World. In 1493, Pope Alexander VI divided the lands discovered by Columbus between two Catholic countries, portioning half to Portugal and half to Spain. In return, Spain and Portugal had the exclusive right and responsibility to convert inhabitants of the New World to Catholicism.

That such a mission was linked to political conquest was unfortunate; however, it was the greatest and most rapid expansion of Christianity the Church had ever seen. Catholicism would spread to Central and South America, North America, and parts of Asia and Africa.

Meanwhile, the monarchs of Portugal and Spain used their missionary mandate to further their own political aims while cleverly freeing up their own armies and civilians. As the secular explorers searched the New

World for its mythical treasures and conquered its territories, the Catholic clergy taught the natives the Christian faith at Catholic missions.

Priests from a variety of orders brought the faith to the vast regions and many peoples of the New World.

In Central and South America, the unwilling natives of Peru, Colombia, Ecuador, Venezuela, Bolivia, and Chile were converted through forceful invasion by Spanish Mercedarians (the order founded in 1218 by St. Peter Nolasco), Dominicans, Franciscans, and Jesuits, followed by Augustinians and Salesians. In a similar manner, Portuguese Jesuits, Franciscans, and Carmelites brought Christianity to the huge territory that would become Brazil, and Spanish Franciscans and Jesuits forcefully converted hundreds of thousands of natives in Central America.

In North America, the Spanish Franciscans, Dominicans, and Jesuits also spread Christianity to the native people in Mexico and the borderlands of Florida, New Mexico, California, Texas, and Arizona. (Fra Junipero Serra is perhaps the most famous Franciscan to work in this huge territory.) French Jesuits, Recollets (French Franciscans), Sulpicians (named after the ecclesiastical writer Sulpicius Severus, who entered into monastic life after his wife's death in A.D. 390), Capuchins, and Carmelites, as well as diocesan priests, also risked their lives to spread Catholicism throughout New France, an area that included Nova Scotia, Acadia, New Brunswick, Quebec, Maine, New York, Illinois, and Louisiana. English missionary efforts also had a hand in this activity, spreading out from the state of Maryland, which was first settled by George Calvert, an English Catholic who sought freedom of religion in the New World.

While some natives accepted conversion peacefully, others did not. In both the eastern and western territories of the United States, many priests endured great hardship. They suffered and died believing it was their duty to bring the Word of God to the people of the New World. Missionaries who were martyred for their faith include the martyrs Isaac Jogues, S.J. (1607–1646), and Jean de Brebéuf (1593–1649). Even as these missionaries faced danger and were martyred, the indigenous people suffered, too, as their safety and well-being were threatened, their lifestyles and value systems invalidated, and their spiritual practices rejected.

≪∘ 24 ∘≫

VATICAN I: LIBERAL TRENDS CRITICIZED

From the mid-seventeenth to the mid-nineteenth centuries, the Church in Europe struggled to cope with new ideas, new ideals, and changes in political order. The French Revolution, the demise of monarchies, and the rise of democratically elected governments throughout Europe undermined some of the protection that both Catholic and Protestant churches had previously enjoyed.

Additionally, the hallmarks of the Enlightenment—freedom of thought, rationalism, and liberalism—all challenged the way the Church had always operated. The Church has never been known for hastily changing its beliefs and practices to keep up with political and cultural trends.

Therefore, it isn't surprising that conservative Catholic clergy denounced new ideas and new approaches to interpreting the world. For instance, when books such as *On the Origin of Species* by Charles Darwin challenged long-held views of Creation, the Church hierarchy refused to modify its stand on the literal truth of the creation story in the Old Testament.

Liberalism and freethinking, which were replacing blind obedience to authority, challenged the individual's adherence to the Church. Society was becoming less dogmatic and more secular.

The Catholic Church came to be associated with the old world order, and some governments even adopted an anti-Catholic stand. Many individuals gave up their belief in God. By the middle of the nineteenth century, Catholics in Europe were a fractured and insecure group.

Something had to be done, and Pius IX took control of the task at hand. Pius IX was a strong pope who brought significant changes to the Church throughout his long tenure from 1846 to 1878.

Pius was not an intellectual, and he alienated those who wanted the Church to open up to new scholarly methods and to recognize the new democratic and social movements, including freedom of religious practice. However, he was a pious, personable, charitable, and—above all— charmingly persuasive man committed to the solidarity of the Church.

Pius IX worked hard to help bishops deal with their governments, to relocate the leadership of many religious orders to Rome, and to hold on to the land of the Papal States, despite the newly formed Italian republic's efforts to take it away. He had the courage to stand up to political leaders and to his opponents, and many in the Church rallied around his strength. (In 1870, the Italian leader Garibaldi did reduce the land holdings of the Church to the acreage that is Vatican City, in the heart of Rome. Vatican City is an independent papal state.)

In December 1869, Pius IX called together a general council, known as Vatican I, to promulgate the doctrine of papal infallibility. Despite the protests of liberal prelates who believed the Church should focus on modernization, the conservative views of the pope and his supporters prevailed, and papal infallibility passed the vote.

By the time of Pius's death, the Church was virtually at war with society. However, Pius IX had strengthened the Church internally. The community had regained its piety, and its religious order once again thrived. The importance of the sacraments, the reaffirmation of Christ as both God and man, and a true sense of the supernatural would continue to enlighten the interior life of most Catholics.

It would be nearly a century before the church undertook serious efforts toward modernization (see Number 26, Vatican II: drastic changes).

∞ 25 ∞

UPHEAVAL IN THE LATE NINETEENTH CENTURY AND TWENTIETH CENTURY

The reactionary attitudes that Vatican I established could not help the Church deal with the social and political upheavals of the late nineteenth century and the twentieth century. The Church had to form new policies and groups to deal with the issues of the day.

The Industrial Revolution in the nineteenth century was one of the movements that catapulted Western civilization into the modern age and created many problems, including the oppression of the working class. As the need for industrial labor increased, entire families left farms and small towns to work in mills and factories. Living conditions in large cities became horrendous: Large populations were cooped up in slums, and the working conditions were no better. Workers had no rights and no protection. Child labor was common.

The Church acted to alleviate the suffering of workers during this time by providing social services, bringing religion to workers' lives, and publicly supporting workers' rights. In 1891, Pope Leo XIII issued *Rerum Novarum,* an important encyclical on workers' rights that upheld the right of the individual to private property and defined the family as the primary social unit. It stated that workers had a right to a living wage and the right to organize in order to improve their lot. The *Rerum Novarum* also made it clear that the Church was in favor of trade unions.

In the twentieth century, the popes tried to steer a neutral course through the political maelstroms of fascism, communism, and the two world wars. Benedict XV was totally opposed to World War I and found it completely unjustifiable. However, he maintained neutrality and did not publicly come out against the war for fear that Catholics would be hurt if they emulated his stance. As a result of his neutrality, all sides were angry with him by the end of the war.

Pius XI saw the rise of Hitler and Mussolini and their dictatorships, which posed a threat to the Catholic Church. In the encyclicals he issued, Pius XI denounced the Nazi regime as well as racism and anti-Semitism, but he passed away in February of 1939, before the events of World War II really began to unfold.

Pius XII, his successor, maintained neutrality during World War II. Although he is criticized today for not speaking out strongly enough against the atrocities committed by the Nazis and other fascist regimes, he did some work on relief efforts for the Jews. The Vatican also carried on a massive and expensive war relief effort and launched a huge program to find missing persons.

The Church had weathered many serious world issues by the end of the first half of the twentieth century, and it wouldn't be long into the second half of the century before it underwent sweeping changes of its own from within.

∽ 26 ∽

VATICAN II: DRASTIC CHANGES

The Church experienced its most drastic changes after Pope John XXIII was elected in 1958. Thanks to John XXIII's influence, Catholicism finally modernized. John ushered in a new era of tolerance, openness, and dialogue in the Church by convening a general council that ran for four sessions, from 1962 to 1965. This council is known as Vatican II.

John XXIII set the tone of the council by expressing optimism and belief that all members of the Church, particularly the bishops, could open up dialogue within the Church, with other Christian faiths, and with nonreligious groups everywhere. The goal of all this dialogue was to find areas of common ground and to tackle common problems.

John XXIII asked the bishops from all over the world to set the agenda for the council and to have a share of influence as great as or greater than the Curia in determining issues and exploring directions. At this council, for once, the liberals prevailed. Even though Pope John XXIII died before the council was finished, his successor, Paul VI, carried on in the same spirit.

The Second Vatican Council made many important changes possible. For instance, Liturgy is now conducted in the vernacular language of each church's parishioners and not in Latin, so that the service is accessible to all laypersons, who are now given the opportunity to participate fully.

For centuries, the writings of the Church focused on who had what power over whom. The Church emphasized the importance of hierarchy: pope over bishops, bishops over clergy, clergy over the laity. Since Vatican II, however, the power lies in the common priesthood of the faithful, and the clergy's role is defined as service to the community of the Church. The laity's role was greatly expanded as well.

The Church also changed its outlook toward other Christian denominations as a result of Vatican II. It was no longer the Church's goal to try to convert Protestants back to Catholicism. Instead, the Church recognized the status of all Protestant communities, apologized for contributing to Christian disunity and the mistakes made during the Counter-Reformation (a period of revitalization in the Roman Catholic Church, from the mid-sixteenth century to the time of the Thirty Years' War, 1618–1648) and urged all Christian communities to work together to solve social problems.

Writings that were once accepted as divine revelation to an individual and, consequently, adhered to rigidly, were subject to new interpretations during this time. The Church accepted that written works are always influenced by historical context and may not have as much relevance for succeeding generations.

Rather than expressing skepticism, or even condemnation, of new forms of government or new social movements, the Church is now more open to accepting and embracing them. Its new position is one of service to humanity, and it has become committed to working with all groups for human rights and dignity.

Since Vatican II, the Church has continued to experience a tidal wave of change. The new liturgy, the questioning of the Church's authority, and the changes in the role of priests and other clergy have all rocked the ecclesiastical boat. Along with questioning authority, more Catholics have come to realize the importance of individual conscience and of the moral responsibility people have in making decisions that affect their actions.

Today, controversies around priestly celibacy, birth control, divorce, and the ordination of women continue to fire up ecclesiastical discussions. Is it fair that Catholics cannot remarry after a divorce as long as the first spouse is still alive? Is it wrong to practice birth control when a couple has had as many children as they feel they can handle? The Church as a whole now has more sympathy for people who are in these types of situations. One thing is certain: Dialogue is alive and well in the Church at present.

∞ 27 ∞

AUTHORITY SHIFTS WITHIN THE CHURCH

Vatican II touched off a major revolution within the Church. In the old days, the word that was passed down from the top of the hierarchy was law. But after Vatican II, Catholic clergymen and laypeople were questioning that authority. Forces within the Church wanted decisions to be more democratic. However, there has not been enough support from Church hierarchy for these kinds of changes.

One of the problems that the Church faces as a result of the post–Vatican II changes is the decline in the number of people entering the vocations of priests, nuns, and brothers, which began in the late 1960s and early 1970s. The reason for the decline is not obvious—it's not the vow of celibacy. In fact, there is evidence that the problem lies in the shifting relationship between the clergy and the laity.

After Vatican II, the Church proclaimed the priesthood of all the laity. While this new attitude was beneficial to lay Catholics, who now felt they were more involved with the Church, members of the clergy lost some of their special status as mediators between the laity and God. The increased participation of all the faithful in the sacraments began to impinge on the clergy's ministerial roles.

However, the shift in roles has also been beneficial. The Church began to realize that priests are not superhuman. They need vacations, pension plans, friends they can rely on, and personal interests that invigorate them and allow them, like other human beings, to do a better job. The recognition of priests' humanity and need for support, as well as a strong attempt to help men discern whether they are suited for the priestly role, have helped reduce the isolation experienced by many priests. It has also promoted a healthier, more realistic view of clergy among the laity.

Part 2

ESSENTIAL
BELIEFS

*I*N ADDITION TO BEING A FAITH, CATHOLICISM IS ALSO A SYSTEM of beliefs. The beliefs taught by the Church as being handed down by God are called dogmas. Because the Catholic Church is a living, growing entity, however, these beliefs have been interpreted and shaped by generations of holy men and theologians over the Church's 2,000-year history. Although open to changes that come with the times, the Catholic Church also teaches that these basic dogmas have always been true.

The beliefs taught by the Church that are not dogmas are called doctrines. Doctrines can be changed under new circumstances, and new doctrines can arise from time to time.

The Catholic Church has four basic tenets that apply to its overall system of beliefs: tradition, universality, reason, and analogy.

Tradition includes all the teachings contained in the Bible, while universality is the openness to all truth, unfettered by any particular culture and unrestricted to all human beings.

The last two tenets, analogy and reason, are applied in the quest to understand the Catholic mysteries. Analogy is a common device of logic that helps us understand God through our knowledge of the created world; reason and philosophy are both pre-eminent in the Church's thinking.

❧ 28 ❧

WHAT IS CATECHISM?

Catechism literally means "instruction by word of mouth." Technically speaking, a catechism is a manual of doctrine and a system of instruction written out in questions and answers, used as a fixed and stable scheme of instruction. (This long and well-established tradition dates back to Socrates. The Gospels show how Jesus Christ frequently used questions and answers as part of His method of teaching.) Certainly, when used within parishes for the education of children or converts, catechism is just that. But the catechisms meant for popular use are local versions of an official Catechism written with the genuine authority of the Holy See in Rome. This Catechism is intended for the particular edification of bishops.

The first official Catechism is known as the *Roman Catechism*. Its formulation was begun in 1562, at the Council of Trent, the council that convened in response to the Protestant Reformation crisis, and it was completed in 1564. Issued by St. Pius V, it was intended for priests.

In 1870, after Vatican I, a new work was issued. Later still, in 1962, the Vatican II Council led by Pope John XXIII called for a spirit of renewal and opened a large-scale project that took a new approach to the Catechism. Eventually completed in 1977, it was issued under the aegis of Pope John Paul II.

The prologue of the new Catechism opens with a note of joy: "God, infinitely perfect and blessed in Himself, in a plan of sheer goodness freely created man to make Him share in His own blessed life." From this basic tenet, the Catholic belief system and its instruction follows.

As the Catholic Church is built on tradition, the material is structured in four sections, similar to the Catechism of Pius V. It includes the profession of faith (including the Nicene Creed); the celebration of the Christian mystery (including the liturgy and sacraments); life in Christ (the Catholic way to live, including the Ten Commandments); and Christian prayer (the importance, relevance, and holiness of prayer).

Within these sections, the material is presented in a way that responds to the questions of the time. Every element of Catholic life and beliefs, from apostolic succession to points of moral ambiguity, is addressed.

29

THE DUAL NATURE OF CHRIST: HUMAN AND DIVINE

The most basic of the Church's doctrines is the idea that human beings achieve salvation through divine grace, where divine blessings are an expression of God's love.

God's grace is expressed through the dual nature of Christ (man and God) and the trinity of persons in God (see Number 30). These two mysteries are fundamental to Catholic belief and the Church's teachings about God.

On his deathbed, just before receiving the Holy Eucharist, St. Thomas Aquinas, considered to be one of the fathers of the Church, said: "If in this world there be any knowledge of this sacrament stronger than that of faith, I wish now to use it in affirming that I firmly believe and know as certain that Jesus Christ, True God and True Man, Son of God and Son of the Virgin Mary, is in this Sacrament."

St. Thomas affirms Christ's humanity, that Jesus was born and died a man, with a man's physical strengths and weaknesses. And yet, he also asserts Jesus' divinity, acknowledging that the man who walked among us 2,000 years ago was indeed a divine person, a person of God, who made Himself over into our image for a brief time.

The Catholic Church teaches that it is our great gift that Christ walked among us, was one of us, and took on the burden of atonement for our sins. Catholics believe that the world is essentially good but that it has fallen from grace, or the "divine presence," into original sin. As a result of this falling away, the world has to be redeemed by God in Christ.

Jesus of Nazareth was not the only man who traveled around the countryside preaching sermons and instructing the people in the Way of God. How, then, did His followers come to know He was the Christ? They knew because of the prophecies of the Old Testament and the miracles that Jesus worked when He walked among them.

Jesus' identity was revealed at His baptism. When He arose from the waters of the Jordan, the Heavens opened, "and the Spirit as a dove [descended] upon Him. And a voice came from the Heavens, 'You are my beloved Son; with you I am well pleased'" (Mark 1:11). At this moment, Jesus was proclaimed the Messiah.

It is recorded in the Gospel of John, Chapters 1–11, that Jesus performed thirty-five miracles; of these, seven were "sign miracles" that demonstrated Jesus was the Christ. The first of the sign miracles—and therefore the most important one—was the miracle at the wedding feast in Cana, where Jesus changed water into wine. The other six of Jesus' sign miracles include Jesus healing a royal official's son; healing a paralytic man who had been unable to walk for thirty-eight years; feeding 5,000 people with only five loaves of bread and two fish; walking on the sea to calm His disciples, who were frightened that their boat was sinking; healing a blind man by placing mud mixed with His saliva over his eyes and telling him to wash in a pool; and raising Lazarus from the dead. (This last miracle won over many religious leaders, who began to follow Jesus and His teachings.)

In the view of the Roman Catholic Church, the miracles demonstrate both Christ's compassion and the power of the living God. They are potent symbols that show how Jesus helped His followers understand what He was doing. His miracles persuaded the disciples that Jesus was God's son on Earth. Taking human form did not mean that Jesus was not true God as well, nor is it true that by being God He was any less human, as various heresies taught. The fact that the Son of God was both God and man is one of the central mysteries of the Catholic faith.

The Church explains that through the Incarnation of God into human form, "human nature was assumed, not absorbed" (*Gaudium et spes,* 22:2). Christ had a human body, soul, intellect, and will, which belonged to the divine person, the Son of God, who assumed them. With a truly human soul and knowledge, Christ would have to learn from inquiry and experience like other men. The Church teaches that He loved all mankind with His human heart, which has led to veneration of the Sacred Heart of Jesus.

As divinity, Christ knew and manifested everything that pertained to God. For example, Jesus could know what was in someone's heart (Mark 2:8; John 2:25).

30

THE MYSTERY OF THE HOLY TRINITY

The Catholic Church regards the mystery of the Holy Trinity—three persons in one God—as one of the central mysteries of the faith. It is the mystery about the nature of God Himself and the source of all other mysteries of faith, because God is the source of all Creation.

The Catechism of the Catholic Church describes a mystery as something that is "hidden in God, which can never be known unless . . . revealed by God." It is something that is difficult to comprehend, "that is inaccessible to reason alone," according to the Catechism, yet it is a central article of the Catholic faith.

The knowledge of God's oneness was imparted through divine revelations to men, as recounted in the Old Testament. God told Israel, His chosen nation: "Hear, O Israel! The LORD is our God, the LORD alone! Therefore, you shall love the LORD, your God, with all your heart, and with all your soul, and with all your strength" (Deuteronomy 6:4–5).

God revealed Himself to the people of Israel progressively, over time, but one of the most important revelations for the Old and New Covenants was when He told His divine name to Moses as He appeared to him in the burning bush: "I am who I am. . . . This is my name forever" (Exodus 3:14–15). The divine name is mysterious, and the Church believes it expresses God as infinitely beyond anything man can comprehend.

From the earliest days of the Church, the Apostles referred to the Holy Trinity of God. The Church fathers aided the early Church councils to clarify the theology of the Holy Trinity, and eventually, the Church declared a dogma of the Holy Trinity. (See the Introduction of this section regarding dogma and doctrine; the Church *declares* dogmas and *develops* doctrines.)

The dogma of the Holy Trinity consists of three parts:

1. The Trinity is One. The Church does not believe in three gods, but in one God in three persons. These persons do not share one divinity—each of them is God, completely and utterly.
2. The divine persons are really distinct from one another. Father, Son, and Holy Spirit are not simply names for different aspects of God. Rather, they are distinct persons with distinct origins and special roles. God the Father is Creator or Source; God the Son is Redeemer; God the Holy Spirit is Advocate and Teacher.
3. The divine persons are relative to one another and are distinguished by the ways in which they relate to one another. According to Lateran Council IV (1215), it is the Father who generates, the Son who is begotten, and the Holy Spirit who proceeds. "The Father is related to the Son, the Son to the Father, and the Holy Spirit to both" (Council of Florence, c.1438).

Over time, this belief came to be enshrined in the central worship of the Church, the Eucharistic liturgy. At every Mass, the priest gives this blessing: "The grace of the Lord Jesus Christ, the love of God, and the fellowship of the Holy Spirit be with you all."

God's love is everlasting. "With age-old love I have loved you," God tells His people through Jeremiah (31:3). The Church teaches that God not only loves us, "God is love" (1 John 4:8, 16). According to the Gospel of John, God is an external exchange of love between Father, Son, and Holy Spirit, and human beings are destined to share in that exchange.

⚬⚬ 31 ⚬⚬

DIVINE PROVIDENCE AND FREE WILL

According to the Scriptures, Creation is the work of the Holy Trinity. Having created His work, God is present to all His creatures. "In Him we live, and move and have our being," wrote Saint Augustine. God is with us to uphold and sustain us, enabling us to act and helping us to achieve salvation. Catholics believe that recognizing our total dependence on our Creator is a source of wisdom, joy, and confidence.

Creation is not perfect. The Church speaks of it as being a journey. God guides His creatures on His journey by means of divine providence, His way of governing creation. Scripture teaches that this providence is concrete and immediate, and that God cares for all, from the greatest to the smallest, here and now. Jesus taught His followers not to worry: "So do not worry and say, 'What are we to eat?' or 'What are we to drink?' or

'What are we to wear?' . . . Your Heavenly Father knows that you need them all. But seek first the kingdom [of God] and His righteousness, and all these things will be given you besides" (Matthew 6:31–33).

It requires humility and faith to begin to feel or to draw close to God's power. The Virgin Mary modeled this faith with her words: "Nothing will be impossible with God."

The Catholic faith accepts that God's power is mysterious, and we don't always understand His ways. Human beings often question why God, who created the world and cares for everything in it, allows evil and suffering to exist. The answer to this complicated question lies in the fact that God also granted human beings the free will to act on their own, to make their own decisions, and to interact with each other in the ways that they choose. Physical evil, suffering, disease, and natural calamities exist because the world is still in flux and is not yet perfect. Moral evil, which is considered to be far worse than physical evil, also exists because human beings and angels, both intelligent creatures with free will, have the power to make choices and, hence, to go astray.

It is true that God allows evil and suffering in the world—He even allowed His own Son to suffer and be crucified. However, the Church teaches that God, through His providence, can conquer suffering and bring good from evil, even a moral evil caused by His creatures. From the murder of Christ, caused by the sins of all human beings, God brought about His glorification and the redemption of humankind.

32

GOD THE FATHER

Many religions have an image of God the Father, and the Catholic Church is no exception. It teaches that God is the origin and Creator of all, and He provides protection and loving care for all His children. In the Old Testament, God is called the Father because He created the world. In the imagery of the Book of Exodus, God the Father made a covenant and gave His Laws to Israel, His firstborn son (Exodus 4:22).

The qualities of God as revealed in the Old Testament are mercy and graciousness: "I will not give vent to my blazing anger. . . . For I am God and not man, the Holy One present among you" (Hosea 11:9). When Moses led the Israelites out of Egypt and they later fell to worshiping the gold calf, God heard Moses' prayer and agreed to walk amid the unfaithful to demonstrate His love. "The LORD, the LORD, a merciful and gracious God, slow to anger and rich in kindness and fidelity" (Exodus 34:6).

The Church believes that God is unique and that He made Heaven and Earth. He transcends the world and history, and He is enduring and unchanging. He remains ever faithful. Following the Hebrew Scriptures and tradition, the Church believes that "God is the fullness of Being and of every perfection, without origin and without end. All creatures receive all that they are and have from Him. But He alone is His very being, and He is of Himself everything that He is" (Catechism of the Catholic Church, 1, II, 213).

The God of the Scriptures is also known for His truth. As the Psalms proclaim, "Your every word is enduring; all your just edicts are forever" (Psalms 119:160). The Church teaches that God is truth itself and that He can never deceive, so believers can fully trust in His Word on all matters. God's truth is synonymous with His wisdom, which He can impart to humans through revelation. God, who created Heaven and Earth, knows about everything He created. Anything He reveals is true instruction, and He sent His Son into the world "to testify to the truth" (John 18:37).

The Church teaches that God's sole reason for establishing a covenant with the people of Israel was His pure, unsolicited love. Because of this love, God never stopped saving and forgiving the Israelites. The Scriptures characterize God's love for His people as boundless and everlasting. God's love triumphed over the worst infidelities. His love for us is why God gave us His most precious gift: "God so loved the world that He gave His only Son" (John 3:16).

In the Catholic creed, God is referred to as "the Almighty." This adjective refers to His omnipotence, or universal power and might—God created everything, He rules everything, and He can do everything. His power is loving and mysterious. God reveals His loving power in the way He lovingly takes care of His children, and by His mercy, for He displays His power not by vengeance but by forgiveness.

For the Catholic Church, God is Father because He is the origin of everything and the supreme authority. Additionally, God is a Father in relation to His Son, Jesus Christ.

33

GOD THE SON

The first ecumenical council at Nicaea decreed that the Son is "consubstantial" with the Father; that is, He is one God with Him. Jesus is the "only-begotten" Son of God, "true God from true God, begotten not made" (Nicene Creed).

But what does all this mean, and how does it relate to an understanding of Jesus Christ? Catholics believe that Jesus of Nazareth, the carpenter who was born in Bethlehem during the time of King Herod the Great and who was crucified under the procurator Pontius Pilate, is also the second person of the Trinity. The Gospel of Matthew relates that St. Peter once told Jesus, "You are the Messiah, the Son of the living God" (Matthew 16:16). Catholics believe that Jesus was the Son of the Father; He suffered and died for mankind, arose, and lives with men forever. That message is at the heart of all the Church's teachings.

The Church teaches that Jesus became a man to save humans by reconciling them with God, so that they might know God's love, and also to be a model of holiness. Through imitating Christ and getting close to Him, people could also partake in the divine nature. God's taking of a human form is known as the Incarnation. Incarnation, which literally means "made into flesh," describes what happened when Jesus assumed a bodily form and the human condition. Understanding the concept of the Incarnation is essential to the Catholic belief system.

The name *Jesus* comes from the Hebrew for "God saves." The Church teaches that God was not content only to save the Hebrews from literal slavery or domination by another nation. He also wanted to save them from their sins, and His Son's death atoned for the sins of mankind. Human beings must be aware of their need for salvation and must call on their Redeemer—this is why the name of Jesus is at the heart of all Catholic prayer.

The title *Christ* is the Greek equivalent of the Hebrew *Messiah*, the "anointed one." In Israel, those consecrated to God—including kings, priests, and prophets—were anointed with oil. Jesus was all three: the King of Kings, a priest, and a prophet of the New Kingdom. Many Jews hoped that Jesus was the long-promised Messiah who would free them from literal, or political, bondage, but Christ's kingdom was not a temporal one. As Jesus said to Peter, "The Son of Man did not come to be served but to serve and to give His life as a ransom for many" (Matthew 20:28).

Jesus was also known by the title *Lord*, in recognition of His divine power. As Jesus was both a human and divine being, the Church accepts and believes mysteries of Christ's life that cannot be fully explained. The mysteries of the Incarnation, which have to do with Jesus' early life, include conception by the power of the Holy Spirit, and birth to a virgin, Mary, who is venerated as the Holy Mother of God. The so-called Paschal mysteries, which have to do with the end of Jesus' life, include the Passion, Crucifixion, death, burial, descent into Hell, Resurrection, and Ascension. These two sets of mysteries, revolving around Christmas and

Easter, illuminate the purpose of Jesus' earthly life: the revelation of the Father and the redemption of humankind.

The mysteries of Jesus' early life contain important lessons for the Church:

1. **Jesus' birth in a lowly stable.** One of the conditions for the faithful to enter the Kingdom of God is to humble themselves as children of God.

2. **Jesus' circumcision.** Eight days after His birth, Jesus was circumcised under the covenant of Abraham and was, therefore, subject to the Law that God had given to the Hebrews. The circumcision prefigured Baptism, a sacrament that reminds Catholics they are subject to the Law of God and the teachings of Christ.

3. **The feast of the Epiphany (the arrival of three wise men bearing gifts to the baby Jesus).** The wise men represented neighboring pagan nations who would take up the good news of the Messiah, as was predicted in the Old Testament.

4. **The presentation of the infant Jesus in the temple.** At this time, Simeon and Anna recognized that Jesus was the Savior. Simeon and Anna prefigured all the others who would hear Jesus' words and recognize Him as God.

5. **The flight of the holy family into Egypt and the massacre of the innocents by Herod.** This tragedy characterized the opposition of darkness to light and the kind of persecution Jesus faced

all His life. His followers would also share that persecution with Him.

6. **Mary and Joseph finding Jesus in the temple at the age of twelve, discussing Scriptures with the wise men.** This event foretold His mission—that He must be about His father's business (Luke 2:49).

The Church teaches us that Jesus' entire life, and not just His death, was dedicated to humankind's redemption. By becoming poor, He enriched mankind; as an obedient son, He made up for human beings' disobedience. His words purified the ears of His listeners; His cures and driving out of unclean spirits was His way of taking on men's weaknesses; and His Resurrection justified man's existence. He existed only for human beings' salvation and to be a model for them.

∽∂ 34 ∂∽

GOD THE HOLY SPIRIT

Jesus is considered to be the first Paraclete (advocate), pleading with God on behalf of humankind. Before He returned to Heaven to join the Father, He told His followers that a second Paraclete, the Spirit, would be sent down to dwell with the Apostles in order to guide them and would remain with mankind until Judgment Day. Existing since creation, the

Spirit is the third person of God. According to the Church, people can only draw close to Christ if they have been touched by the Holy Spirit, who gives His grace through the sacrament of Baptism.

The Church recognizes God the Father as the source of all divinity. Therefore, the Holy Spirit, the third person of the Trinity, is one with and equal to God the Father and the Son. They are all of the same substance and have the same nature. In 1438, the Council of Florence explained, "The Holy Spirit is eternally from Father and Son; He has His nature and subsistence at once from the Father and the Son. He proceeds eternally from both as from one principle and through one spiration."

The Spirit works invisibly. He inspired the prophets, and now He inspires other aspects of the faith, such as the sacraments, which put the faithful into communion with Christ; prayer, in which He intercedes for the faithful; ministries and missions; and the saints, through whom He shows His holiness.

The Holy Spirit has a joint mission with Christ. The world has seen Christ, but it is the Spirit who revealed Him. Christ was anointed, but it was the coming upon Him of the Spirit that was His anointing. Christ and the Spirit are inseparable. When Christ ascended to Heaven, He sent the Holy Spirit to dwell among mankind to unite all to Christ as adopted children. At Pentecost, the Spirit descended on the Apostles, and He has remained with the Church ever since. The Church completes the mission of Christ and the Holy Spirit because in a mysterious way the Church is the Body of Christ as well as the Temple of the Holy Spirit.

The Spirit works in many ways, preparing human beings through grace to draw them to Christ; manifesting the Risen Lord to human beings by spreading His word and helping them to understand the mysteries of the faith; making Christ present, especially in the Eucharist; and bringing human beings into closeness with God.

❧ 35 ❧

The names and symbols of the Spirit

In the Old Testament, there were two streams of prophecy: one for the Messiah and one for the Holy Spirit. The Spirit spoke of Himself through the prophets: "But a shoot shall sprout from the stump of Jesse, and from his roots a bud shall blossom. The spirit of the LORD shall rest upon him: a spirit of wisdom and of understanding, A spirit of counsel and of strength, a spirit of knowledge and of fear of the LORD" (Isaiah 11:1–2).

The last prophet through whom the Holy Spirit spoke was John the Baptist. John said of Christ, "On whomever you see the Spirit come down and remain, He is the one who will baptize with the Holy Spirit" (John 1:33–36). After baptism, Christ entered into His joint mission with the Holy Spirit. He alluded to the Spirit as He preached to the crowds, as He spoke to Nicodemus and the Samaritan woman, and as He talked to His disciples about prayer and their future testament to Him.

There are many titles that describe the Holy Spirit. As previously mentioned, the Spirit is known as *Paraclete*, which is commonly translated as "consoler," "advocate," or "he who is called to one's side." He is also known as the Spirit of Truth, the Spirit of the Promise, the Spirit of Adoption, the Spirit of Christ, the Spirit of the Lord, and the Spirit of God.

Many symbols are also connected to the Holy Spirit:

Water: Man's birth takes place in water, and the water of Baptism signifies rebirth.

Oil: The action of anointing with oil relates to Jesus' anointing with the Holy Spirit. Jesus was the Anointed One, revealed and anointed with the power and presence of the Holy Spirit.

Fire: Fire symbolizes the transforming energy of the Holy Spirit, who at Pentecost rested on the heads of the disciples as tongues of fire.

Clouds and light: In the Old Testament, images of clouds and light depicted the Holy Spirit revealing and obscuring God in His apparitions to Moses.

Seal: A symbol of the effect of anointing with the Holy Spirit, an indelible character printed on the soul.

Hand: A reference to the laying on of hands in healing and teaching, where the Holy Spirit is an agent.

Finger: By the finger of the Holy Spirit, Jesus casts out demons and writes on the human heart.

Dove: At Jesus' baptism, the Holy Spirit comes over Him in the form of a dove.

∞ 36 ∞

DEVELOPMENT OF CATHOLIC CANON LAW

The canon law (from the Greek *kanon*, "rule") of the Catholic Church comprises a system of laws and regulations used in governing the vast organization of the Catholic Church and its followers. It encompasses the beliefs (or creeds) of the Church as well. (The term *canon* is also used in reference to the accepted books of the Bible.)

Canon law did not magically appear at the dawn of Christianity, handed down to the Church to be accepted and practiced without question. The Church had to develop canon law for itself. In fact, it has taken the Church just about 2,000 years to study and interpret the Word of Christ as it has been recorded in the Scriptures and to build up the canon of law through deep religious and philosophical inquiry, debate, and even controversy. Throughout this struggle for understanding, the guidance of the Holy Spirit and the leadership of the pope have aided the Church.

The Church recognizes three eras of canon law development.

The era of ancient law lasted from the dawn of Christianity to the twelfth century, ending with Johannes Gratian's publication of his exhaustive canonical work, the *Decretum*. Gratian, a monk and a scholar who was born in Tuscany in the twelfth century, is considered the founder of the "science" of canon law. Gratian undertook the project of compiling Church canon law while he was teaching at a convent in Bologna.

In the *Decretum,* Gratian included not only Church laws that were already in force, but also principles from the extensive group of canon law collected from the earliest days. Covering jurisdiction, historical information, and liturgical practices, Gratian's impressive treatise remained the principal text of Church canon law until the Council of Trent (1545–1563).

The Council of Trent, which convened to tackle the controversies of its era—namely the Reformation—established new laws and principles where confusion had reigned. The Council passed and recorded many rulings, including the affirmation of Divine Tradition, which reflects the belief that Catholic faith is based on scripture and *also* on tradition; the importance of *both* good works and faith in the struggle for salvation; and the actual presence of Christ in the Eucharist. The Council of Trent also standardized the prayers and rituals of the Mass. Those things would remain the same until Vatican II in the 1960s. Since the Council of Trent, the modern era of canon law has lasted through the present.

Although many changes in Catholic canon law took place through the work of specially convened councils like the Nicaean Council and the Council of Trent, the pope also has the power and the authority to issue pontifical laws through apostolic letters (also known as papal bulls). In 1917, Pope Benedict XV issued his comprehensive Code of Canon Law. This was regarded as the canonical authority in the Catholic Church until 1983, when Pope John Paul II issued a new Code of Canon Law, by which Catholics are ruled today. Finally, laws may be passed on a local level, through local ecclesiastical councils, as long as the decisions are made in conformity with Church law.

It's important to understand that changes in canon law do not constitute a rejection of previously held beliefs. Although canon law has endured debate and subsequent shifts in emphasis to better explain the Lord's Word, the Church teaches that these changes occur because of the vitality and organic nature of the faith.

∽∽ *37* ∽∽

EXCOMMUNICATION: SEVERE SIN AGAINST CHURCH LAW

Once Catholics have been baptized and have accepted the authority of the Church, they become full members and must adhere to Church law. But what happens if a Catholic is lax in his or her duty, or rejects some of the beliefs outright? The Church is not hard on those who are negligent, but it also recognizes three formal types of sin against Church law: heresy, apostasy, and schism. These formal transgressions draw the severe penalty of excommunication, which means exclusion from the Church and prohibition from receiving the sacraments. Excommunication is a type of shunning, and it bears severe social stigma.

Heresy is the rejection of a belief at the core of Roman Catholicism. In the early days of the Church, all non-Catholics were considered to be heretics. In recent years, however, the Church has taken a greater interest in charity toward its neighbors and no longer bandies the word *heretic* around.

Apostasy is a much more serious transgression. It is the total repudiation of everything that has to do with Catholicism. It is a lonely route to go, and usually only occurs if a Catholic has profound doubts or undergoes a traumatic experience that leads him or her to reject the Catholic faith. Those who abandon their faith are automatically considered to be outside the Church, but they are not formally charged unless they call public attention to their repudiation.

Interestingly, the Church recognizes three distinct forms of apostasy: when a Catholic layperson abandons his or her faith, when a cleric sheds the ecclesiastical state, and when a member of a religious order abandons the religious state he or she once embraced.

The word *schism* refers to a refusal within the faith to submit to the authority of the Roman pontiff and to recognize the primacy of the pope. Orthodox Churches that broke with Rome in 1054 were referred to as schismatic, for example. Today, there are actually a number of marginal groups within the Church that challenge papal authority on certain issues.

Excommunication doesn't necessarily require a public notice. According to Church law, once a person accepts a heresy or apostasy, or joins a schismatic group, he or she is automatically in a state of excommunication and should no longer partake of the sacraments. In serious cases, however, the Vatican does issue a formal decree of excommunication.

The Church does offer means of reconciliation. Lifting an excommunication requires approval from a bishop, although he will often delegate the commission to a priest or confessor at his cathedral. In matters of a truly serious nature, though, it is not easy to obtain reconciliation.

THE STRUCTURE OF CHURCH HIERARCHY

The hierarchy of the Catholic Church is composed of the pope, bishops, priests, and deacons, all of whom are ordained and dedicated to ministry to the faithful. Through dioceses and parishes, they teach and confer the sacraments.

At the top of the hierarchy, which is essentially a pyramid, is the pope. As supreme pontiff and Bishop of Rome, the pope follows a tradition that dates back to St. Peter and the earliest days of the Church. The pope is believed to be infallible when speaking on matters of faith or morals, although he generally consults his advisory body, the College of Cardinals, before he makes a decision affecting the Church.

The hierarchical structure of the Church has existed in more or less the same form since the twelfth century, when Pope Gregory VII instituted many reforms that increased papal control over the Church as a whole. One such reform did away with lay investiture, which meant that public officials and monarchs lost the right to invest (or endow him with power) a bishop in their diocese. From then on, only the pope had the right to appoint a bishop, and in turn the bishops reported only to the pope. Gregory's aim in passing this reform was to prevent secular control over the Church's properties and activities.

At about the same time, the Church began to recognize the power of canon law, which codified all Church activities and dealt with questions ranging from who could administer a sacrament to how the pope was chosen. The Code of Canon Law determined procedures that were to be followed in Church governance, and clearly structured and supported the hierarchical framework.

The College of Cardinals usually elects the pontiff from among their membership. Once the pope is chosen, he remains the head of the Catholic Church until his death. As well as being the chief bishop of the Roman Catholic Church, the pope is also the ruler of Vatican City, which allows him to have independence from any earthly political jurisdiction.

The cardinals, who have the authority to elect and advise the pope, occupy the next step down on the hierarchical pyramid of Church governance. All cardinals are ordained bishops (see Number 39). They keep their episcopal sees (their official seats of authority), whether they are residential or titular (that is, whether they are bishops of an actual place, such as the archdiocese of Chicago, or honorary bishops, by title only), along with their responsibilities as bishops. There are three levels of cardinals:

1. Cardinal bishops, or Episcopal cardinals
2. Cardinal priests, or presbyter cardinals
3. Cardinal deacons, or diaconal cardinals

The cardinal bishops are the titular bishops of the seven suburban sees of Rome. They elect a dean and subdean from their members. The dean presides over the college, with the subdean acting in his absence, making them the second- and third-highest-ranking clerics in the Church.

Cardinal priests are the ordinary bishops of dioceses who have been made cardinals. Cardinal deacons are titular archbishops who work for the Roman Curia and have been raised to the cardinalate. Together, the cardinals make up the Sacred College of Cardinals, which acts as an advisory body to the pope.

The cardinal bishops work full-time in the Roman Curia. The Curia is the central body of the Church, subdivided into departments that handle such matters as canon law, heresies, the election and governance of bishops and dioceses, administration of the sacraments, matters concerning religious orders, missionary work, rites and liturgies, ceremonies, and religious studies. Certain departments of the Curia also make decisions regarding special petitions to the Curia, such as annulment petitions.

∾ 39 ∾

THE ROLE OF BISHOPS

The word *bishop* comes from the Greek, meaning inspector, overseer, or superintendent. In the writings of the early Church, the terms *bishop* (*episcopes*) and *priest* (*presbyter*) were interchangeable. However, as early as the second century A.D., Christians began to distinguish between these two roles. "Priests of the second grade" became priests as they are known today; "priests of the first grade" evolved into bishops.

Bishops fulfilled the high priestly roles exemplified by Christ: They were priests, prophets, and kings. As a priest, each bishop had the power to consecrate, offer the Eucharistic Sacrifice, and forgive sins. As a prophet, he had the authority to teach. As a king, he had primary pastoral responsibility to guide his flock. At consecration, he received special graces to equip him for his office.

The power of bishops waned in the twelfth century as they lost some of their independence to the pope. At that time, the bishop became a kind of papal legate, an official representative of the pope in his diocese. Power and authority were highly concentrated in the pope and the Curia.

Since Vatican II, the bishops' role has gained importance through efforts to empower them in their dioceses, in national gatherings, and in worldwide councils or synods. Bishops share their leadership roles with the pope, who is the Bishop of Rome. The bishops' empowerment serves as a balancing force to the central control of the Curia.

Today, the pope still decides who will be made a bishop. However, local councils of bishops are encouraged to help the pope make the decision by giving him their recommendations. Church tradition prescribes that candidates for the position of bishop should have integrity, piety, prudence, and a zeal for souls. They should be trained in theology or canon law, and may not marry (as is true for all priests).

Archbishops, or metropolitans, are the highest bishops. They have authority over an ecclesiastical province and over the bishops within that province. The bishops who report to them are known as suffragans. As part of their obligations, metropolitans must convene provincial synods to make laws and decisions for the province.

Bishops proper preside over dioceses. Each diocese is broken into districts of parishes administered by archpriests or deans.

In some cases, bishops report directly to the pope and are known as exempt bishops. Titular bishops are consecrated, and have a title belonging to a diocese, but they have no jurisdiction in that diocese. They may function as auxiliary bishops or coadjutors (assistants) to diocesan bishops. The *praelati nullius cum territorio separato* heads up a territory that does not belong to a designated diocese. This type of bishop has bishops' governing rights over an area that does form part of a diocese.

Bishops also have assistants. Chief among them is the vicar-general. Furthermore, bishops are advised by a council or chapter composed of canons—priests affiliated with the cathedral. Bishops need the approval of these priests to proceed in certain matters.

A bishop's most basic role is to govern his diocese in spiritual and temporal affairs. Bishops can adopt and enforce the observance of Church laws that those in their diocese must follow. Bishops also are the principal preachers in their dioceses and must personally preach the Word of God to their people, which means they must offer Mass on Sundays and major feast days. They also are expected to reside within the diocese for most of the year, and be present at their churches during Advent, Christmas, Lent, Easter, Pentecost, and Corpus Christi. Bishops are expected to visit the entire dioceses over a five-year period.

Then, every five years, bishops must submit reports on the state of their dioceses to the pope. At the same time, each bishop travels to Rome to visit the Holy Father and to worship at the tombs of Peter and Paul.

PRIESTS AS MEDIATORS BETWEEN GOD AND PEOPLE

Priests are intended to serve as mediators between God and people. In the Catholic Church, there are two degrees of priests: The bishop, who is in a sense a high priest, possessing all the powers of the priesthood and in control of divine worship, and the priests of the second degree, who are most often affiliated with a parish. Every priest has the power to offer the Sacrifice of the Mass, forgive sins, bless, preach, and fulfill all liturgical obligations and priestly functions not reserved to the bishop.

In the early days of the Church, all priests (or presbyters) belonged to a council that looked after the affairs of the Church, which included liturgy and worship, and they worked together in cities under the supervision of the bishop. As the Church grew and spread to suburban and rural areas, priests were assigned to reside in parishes and to look after the spiritual needs of the faithful. Those priests could no longer work closely with the bishop. However, the bishop had authority over them, as their parishes were part of his diocese and subject to his jurisdiction. This arrangement persists in the Church today.

Priests may be diocesan or parish priests, or they may be ordained through a religious order. A pastor or parish priest has the role and duty known as cure of souls (*Cura animarum*). His job is to nurture the spiritual welfare of Church members by preaching, bestowing the sacraments, and supervising and counseling his parishioners in matters of faith and morals, as well as any other concerns they bring to him. He is also supposed to provide religious instruction (especially to the young), usually has a certain number of souls to look after (that is, the Catholic population of his parish), and gets a salary for his work.

Canon law obliges parish priests to say Mass for their flock on Sundays and designated holy days. If a priest's parish becomes too large or duties too numerous, the bishop may appoint an assistant or auxiliary priest or priests to help him.

A rector heads a church not officially designated as a parish and has the same rights and responsibilities as a parish priest. The term may also apply to priests who preside over missions, or to the heads of universities, seminaries, colleges, and religious houses of men.

In addition to priests, deacons are other ordained Church ministers. Their role in the Church appears below that of priests on the hierarchical pyramid. Today, most men who are deacons are on their way to becoming priests. However, the Church once had a permanent deaconate, in which deacons fulfilled specific functions, such as assisting the priest at Mass and other liturgies, reading the Gospel, and preparing the altar for Mass.

Some pastors are irremovable. They cannot be transferred unless there is a serious reason, such as violation of a canonical or criminal law. Other pastors or rectors are movable, but a bishop would usually need a good reason to transfer a priest against his will.

Vatican II took it upon itself to diminish the cultlike status of priests and return them to their original roles in the community. In the Decree on the Ministry and the Life of Priests, Vatican II declared that all the faithful are part of the priesthood, and that the priest is there to serve the faithful just as all the faithful are there to serve each other.

Vatican II recommended that priests be prepared and educated to serve in the community. As well as administering the sacraments and preaching, priests were called upon to act as teachers and examples among the faithful, to lead the faithful in various ministries, and to cultivate the appropriate interpersonal skills.

∽∾ 41 ∽∾

THE JOURNEY OF THE SOUL

Over the course of their lives, human beings are born, grow up, mature, grow old, and die. The cycle of life is the same for all life on Earth—for animals and plants as well as for human beings. What separates humans is our awareness of death and our ability to choose to do good during our limited time on Earth.

Unlike some Eastern religions, the Church does not accept the idea of reincarnation of souls: "It is appointed that human beings die once," wrote Paul (Hebrews 9:27). Human beings have only one lifetime during which to get close to God. This creates a sense of urgency, to do good and acquire grace while one is alive, because after death, people can no longer make choices regarding their destiny.

Death is one of the evils attendant on man in his fallen state; it entered the world on account of sin, as is described in the Book of Genesis. However, death is the gateway to everlasting life. For Christians, therefore, death is also positive, for it is through death, shared with us by Christ, that we can also share in His glory.

The Church does not believe in predestination. Human beings have free will to choose to live a life of virtue or to turn away from God and live a life of sin. God is merciful and will forgive even the most grievous of sins up to the last minute of a person's life—provided the person is truly repentant. However, hardened sinners who do not seek repentance cannot take advantage of God's mercy.

Death brings a separation of the soul from the body, but it is not an end of existence. Depending on how a person has lived his or her life, the soul will go to one of three places: to Heaven, to experience the vision of God; to purgatory, for a purification process before being allowed the vision of God; or to Hell, where he or she will be denied the vision of God. (See Numbers 43, 44, and 45 for more about these three states of being). At the final judgment (the end of the world), also known as the Parousia or Second Coming of Christ, all the just will be reunited with their glorified bodies, to live forever in glory with God.

The Church encourages people to prepare themselves for the hour of their death. The ancient Litany of the Saints contains the petition, "From a sudden and unforeseen death, deliver us, O Lord." St. Joseph is the patron saint of the happy death, and in the Hail Mary, one of the most popular Catholic prayers, Catholics beseech Mary to "pray for us now and at the hour of our death."

Through the sacrament of Baptism, the Christian has already identified with Christ's death. Those who die in Christ's grace share His death
more completely—they become totally incorporated in Him.

THE CATHOLIC UNDERSTANDING OF JUDGMENT

The Church teaches that there are two kinds of judgments—particular
and final. According to Catholic dogma, God makes a particular judgment of each individual's soul immediately after death, when there is a
reckoning of his or her deeds and intentions.

The parable of Lazarus and the rich man, which appears in the Gospel
of Luke, exemplifies particular judgment. According to the story, when
he was alive, the beggar Lazarus would sit outside the rich man's gate and
ask for scraps of food that fell from the man's table. After both men died,
Lazarus went to Heaven as a reward for his humility. Because the rich
man ignored Lazarus and didn't show compassion for a fellow human
being, he went to Hell, where he begged Lazarus to dip his finger in water
and give him a cooling drop. Each man got what he deserved.

In Catholic teaching, the concept of Final (or Last) Judgment applies
to all souls. At this point, "both the just and the unjust" will rise from
the dead and be reunited with their bodies. When Christ "comes in His
glory . . . He will separate them one from another." The evil will "go off

to eternal punishment, but the righteous to eternal life" (Matthew 25:31–32, 46).

When the Resurrection, or restoration, of the body takes place, the blessed in Heaven will have the same bodies as they did on Earth, but those bodies will have special characteristics. Splendor will give bodies a supernatural radiance and make them beautiful to behold. Agility will enable the glorified body to move through space in an instant. Subtlety will allow the complete subordination of the body to the soul, so that both are perfectly integrated. And impassibility will make it impossible for the glorified body to suffer. Also, basic human needs, such as eating or sleeping, will no longer be necessary.

According to St. Augustine, who wrote about the Last Judgment in one of his sermons, at this point each person's relationship with God will become transparent, and the consequences of what he or she did in their earthly lives will be revealed, down to the smallest detail.

The Church teaches that the Last Judgment will also bring revelation and understanding to the minds of human beings, who will then comprehend the full meaning of Creation, salvation, and the mystery of God's providence. Finally, it is a vindication of faith in God and will show how God's justice triumphs over any earthly injustice, because God's love is stronger than death.

The concept of the Last Judgment is meant to inspire a healthy respect for God and His justice and to encourage human beings to repent while they still have time. It is also meant to inspire the hope of God's coming.

The Church teaches that only God knows when Christ will return in glory and the Last Judgment will occur. At that time, Christ will pronounce the final word on all history, and the renewal of the world, together with the restoration of the body, will complete God's plan.

∞ 43 ∞

THE NATURE OF HEAVEN

The Church teaches that those who die in God's grace and are purified get to see God as He is, face-to-face, and live with Christ forever. This communion of life and love with the Trinity, the Virgin Mary, the angels, and all blessed souls is Heavenly—the ultimate object of the deepest human desire and the state of supreme happiness.

By His death and Resurrection, Jesus Christ opened Heaven to all who choose to accept it. Good people benefit fully from Christ's redemption. Those who have believed in Him and have remained faithful become partners in His glory.

The Church's view of Heaven and salvation is certainly not limited to just Catholics and Christians, however. The Church also teaches that anyone who seeks truth and does God's will, insofar as he or she understands it, can be saved, despite ignorance of the Gospels and of the Church.

In Heaven, human beings live with and in Christ, yet still retain their true identity. God is the primary object of a human being's mind and will in Heaven. Once there, individuals receive "beatific vision"—the ability to see God in all His glory. The secondary object of the beatific vision is the knowledge and love of people who Christians have known on Earth.

The essential element in the state of heavenly glory is union with the Blessed Trinity in mind and heart. All who die in the state of grace possess essential glory as soon as their purification is completed. However, the fullness of glory is achieved when people regain their bodies after the Second Coming.

Some theologians speak of Heaven as a state of ultimate happiness in union with God. They explain that we exist to give God glory and to find our happiness, but we find our happiness only in giving glory to God. In Heaven, the members of Christ's Mystical Body glorify God by their participation in the glory of Christ—it is only in Christ that they can do so. Christ is the final temple where God is perfectly adored, and Heaven is its sanctuary. In the state of perfect bliss, physical satisfaction is not the concern; true contentment comes from fulfilling the noble aspirations of the soul. The infinite perfection of the Blessed Trinity and the infinite love of God provide never-ending satisfaction. This happiness does not grow tiresome because it is not mixed with material pleasure, which, by its nature, cannot last. The happiness of Heaven is permanent; there can be no anxiety that it will diminish or go away.

The Catholic Church teaches that heavenly bliss varies from one person to another, in correspondence to the state of the individual's union with God at the time of death. Members enjoy the Company of the Elect—each of the blessed takes delight in the others. Martyrs, virgins, and teachers of the faith receive a special mark or halo that denotes their dedication to Christ or His work during their lifetime.

Because Christ and Mary are now glorified in body, and because a body requires a place in which to dwell, Church tradition follows Scripture in teaching that Heaven is a place. However, it will exist in the fullest sense only after the Parousia, when those who are saved regain their original bodies.

Ultimately, however, the way in which Heaven functions remains a mystery to human beings. Since it is far beyond comprehension, the Scriptures describe it through images and metaphors to which human beings can relate. Life, light, peace, wedding feast, wine of the kingdom, the Father's house, the heavenly Jerusalem, and paradise are just some of the terms used to describe Heaven.

∞ 44 ∞

WHAT ARE PURGATORY AND LIMBO, AND WHY DO CATHOLICS BELIEVE IN THEM?

Although Heaven and Hell might be familiar concepts, purgatory is, perhaps, less well known. It is where those who die in a state of grace and who have the love of God in their hearts go for purification. The Church believes that in purgatory, souls worthy of eternal salvation make expiation for unforgiven venial sins or receive punishment for venial and mortal sins that were forgiven in life.

Although no one can dictate to God, the Church believes that the prayers and intentions of the faithful help God to speed the journey of souls through purgatory. The Church also recommends that the living faithful give alms, practice indulgences, and undertake penitential acts on behalf of the dead: "Why would we doubt that our offerings for the dead bring them some consolation? Let us not hesitate to help those who have died and to offer our prayers for them," writes the great orator St. John Chrysostom in his homily on 1 Corinthians 41:5.

The Church formulated its doctrine on purgatory at the first and second council of Lyons and at the councils of Florence and Trent. Although purgatory is not specifically mentioned in the Bible, belief in its existence has grown because of doctrines regarding divine judgment, the forgiveness of sins, the mercy of God, and the temporal punishment due to sin found in both the Old and the New Testaments. (The Israelites believed that living brethren needed to pray for God to show the departed His mercy.)

Beyond the basic beliefs described above, the nature of purgatory is hard to define. No one knows how much time souls need to spend in purgatory, because the souls live in Aevum, not in worldly time. During that period, the soul becomes highly aware of its failings and transgressions, and is totally focused on reparation.

The nature of the punishment is not completely known either. Some theologians hold that the temporary deprivation of the beatific vision, the longing for a God so near and yet so far, has to be the primary punishment of purgatory.

Some theologians also postulate that there must be a more positive punishment that frees the souls of their sins and brings them closer to God. The point is not the punishment itself (although the Church does maintain that punishment is received), but the intent of punishment—to transform the soul to a state of wholeness and purity so that it is fit to behold God.

While purgatory is a concept that the Church upholds, the Church has no official position on the concept of limbo, which once served to allay the fears of parents whose children died before being baptized. In the past, Catholics believed that unbaptized souls could not gain access into Heaven and, therefore, went to Hell. Although Catholic parents rushed their babies to church for Baptism shortly after birth, some still died without receiving Baptism.

Catholics could not accept the idea that God would subject innocent babies to the fires of Hell because of this, so they reasoned that babies must go to another place—limbo (from the Latin for "border").

Although the exact origins of this teaching are uncertain, Catholics were taught about this third possible eternal location for a long time. For a while, theologians discussed whether the infants experienced any kind of pain, but this idea lasted only until the thirteenth century. Catholics then settled on the idea that limbo is a place where infant souls dwell in natural bliss, if not exactly the true joy of being in the presence of the Lord. However, Church canon law does not include any mention of limbo, and so eventually this idea was rejected. The new Catechism of the Catholic Church does not mention limbo at all.

HELL AS ETERNAL SEPARATION FROM GOD

Hell is a place or state in the afterlife reserved for unbelievers and Catholics who die unrepentant in a state of mortal sin. Forgoing repentance, an individual chooses to exclude himself from God and His grace. If he dies in this state, he is denied the vision of God and communion with the blessed for eternity.

The word *Hell* is derived from the Germanic *hel* ("realm of the dead"). This word was not used in the Old Testament. Rather, the Old Testament counterpart was "Gehenna," an actual place near the territories of the tribes of Judah and Benjamin, where human sacrifices were offered to Canaanite gods Baal and Moloch. Jewish thinking was that the remains of those who turned against Yahweh would lie there. (This idea of Gehenna remained prevalent in Jesus' time.)

In the New Testament, Jesus speaks of Gehenna and of the unquenchable fire, where those who refuse to believe or repent will be sent. Jesus declares that He will "send His angels, and they will collect . . . all who cause others to sin and all evildoers. They will throw them into the fiery furnace" (Matthew 13:41–42). Jesus then will condemn them by saying, "Depart from me, you accursed, into the eternal fire!" (Matthew 25:41). This vivid apocalyptic imagery is meant to dramatize the urgency of the Kingdom and the serious attitude toward salvation that Christians needed to have.

According to the Apostles' Creed, Jesus' own descent into Hell was to the underworld, Sheol, where He met those who had died before Him, to share His victory over death. He died and stayed among the dead for a short time.

Teachings about Hell serve as a warning for human beings to make the best use of their time on Earth. No one is predestined to go to Hell. It is an act of free will to choose mortal sin, to turn away from God, and to persist in that stance. The Missal contains prayers whereby the Church prays for the mercy of God, who wants all to repent. "Grant us your peace in this life, and save us from final damnation" (Roman Missal, EPI, Roman Canon, 88).

The Church holds that immediately after death, those who die in mortal sin descend into Hell, where they suffer eternal fire. The concept of fire in Hell is figurative, however. The chief punishment of Hell is eternal separation from God, because only by seeing God can human beings possess the life and happiness for which they were created. Ultimately, Hell is self-annihilation: Rejection of God is the rejection of the state of being and the choosing of a condition of nonbeing.

∽∽ 46 ∽∽

STRIVING TO BE BETTER—
AND BEING FORGIVEN FOR SHORTCOMINGS

Catholicism is a demanding religion. Its principles—rooted in the Church's understanding of the Word of God—require that Catholics constantly strive to be the best they possibly can be. Although no human being is perfect, it helps to have a strong moral compass, and this entails building the right state of mind. This is one reason why prayer is central to the life of a Catholic.

When it comes to prayer, some people have a mental image of someone kneeling by their bedside or at an altar with hands folded, but it is rarely the norm. In reality, prayer is often a private, personal act that involves simply having a conversation with God, going over some thoughts in communion with Him, or reciting a Rosary and reflecting on the mysteries (see Number 79 for more on the Rosary). It can be the Our Father at the end of the day before bed, or it might be a line thrown out to the Almighty on the way to work. Through prayer, Catholics keep returning to the teachings of Christ (and of the Church), and this gives them strength to deal with others and the stresses of daily life in general.

Prayer is much like meditation. It is a peaceful, calming way of counting blessings and giving thanks. It can also help individuals to sort out their decision-making processes and reset their moral compasses. At the heart of prayer is the act of celebrating the Eucharist (see Number 50).

The Eucharist brings Catholics closer to the divine and draws them out of themselves, because it is a public act. Trying to be a good Catholic can be humbling, but God's mercy shines through, especially at Mass. Partaking of the Body of Christ is healing and inspiring. It helps return Catholics to the path, inspirited to go about their daily lives in a healthful way—and, of course, as part of a community.

Catholicism teaches that no matter how often human beings fail, God is all-forgiving. This forgiveness is a tremendous gift to daily life. It means that when people are distracted, troubled, or harassed, or when they fail to live up to the highest principles, they can still pick themselves up and go on.

What's more, with God's loving mercy, human beings can go on feeling emboldened to try to behave better. This forgiveness gives courage, strength, and support in a way nothing else ever could. It helps make Catholics better citizens in the world as well as better citizens in Christ.

∽ 47 ∽

BELIEF IN SALVATION THROUGH FAITH AND GOOD WORKS

Salvation means overcoming sin and the basic flaws of the human condition, and returning to the ultimate, longed-for state of spirituality. Christ's Resurrection, in which He was transformed into a new mode of existence, is the prime example of salvation. That transformation is what all Catholics are striving to achieve.

When it comes to achieving salvation, the Church has vacillated between emphasis on faith—salvation achieved through private worship—and emphasis on good works. Clearly, it takes a combination of both things to be a good Catholic and to live life as Christ wished us to do.

For Catholics, the constant effort to *be* good and the impulse to *do* good go hand-in-hand. In recent years, the concept of *random acts of kindness* has worked its way into the collective consciousness. This secular idea has long been fostered by the Church. Helping out and spending time with the less fortunate, the sick, and those struggling with problems are all useful efforts in the scheme of the mission, service to others.

Kindness and thoughtfulness toward others exemplify the true meaning of the word *charity*. These things are also at the heart of what it means to be part of a community. Catholics seek to make life better for others, and as such, they look to cultivate generosity of spirit, whether that means teaching, giving money, or helping those in need. Not only is charity unbelievably rewarding; more important, it knits Catholics into the community of the world.

In addition to individual initiatives—for example, foundations established for purposes such as removing asbestos from housing developments or lobbying for arms control—there are at least 1,400 Catholic charitable organizations operating in the United States. They serve 18 million people and include such agencies as the Catholic Health Association, with its 600 hospitals and 300 long-term care facilities, and the Campaign for Human Development, which works to help the poor. This organization collaborates with 200 smaller chapters of antipoverty groups, whose efforts aim to improve laws affecting low-income individuals. Catholic education—another way in which believers actively bring their belief into daily life—is also important to the faith, and numerous Catholic elementary schools, high schools, colleges, and universities operate all over the United States and Canada. (See Number 97.)

Ultimately, to be a Catholic, it is not enough to observe the outward signs of worship only. That falls short of achieving the state of inner worship that is critical to becoming one with the Lord. It is also not enough to do good works alone. No matter how generous Catholics are with their time, they must still observe the obligations of worship that membership in the Church requires.

It is every Catholic's individual responsibility to work out his or her salvation, and the framework of the Church provides plenty of help for every Catholic to reach that goal. As the bishops proclaimed at Vatican II, the values that we cherish on Earth—"human dignity, brotherly communion, and freedom"—are of "vital concern to the kingdom of God."

Strengthened in purpose by faith, it is every Catholic's responsibility to permeate society and to try to be a force for good. As the Catholic Catechism attests, "If a bad apple affects the good ones, cannot we as Christians and Catholics reverse the procedure and be the good ones that affect the bad?"

Part 3
THE
SACRAMENTS

ONE OF THE THINGS THAT DISTINGUISHES THE CATHOLIC FAITH from other religious traditions is strong focus on sacramentality—that is, the belief that God is reflected and present in everything in creation. In the Catholic Church, the seven sacraments are known as instruments of faith because through words and symbols they instruct people in the faith, nourishing, strengthening, and expressing it. Through the sacraments, Catholics profess the ancient faith of the Apostles. For this reason, the sacramental rites cannot be changed or modified. Not even the highest level of Church authority can arbitrarily change them. These unique, enduring traditions provide a means of developing deeper understanding and a framework for marking some of the most important milestones in life.

SACRAMENTALS: GOD REVEALED IN ALL THINGS

In the Catholic worldview, God is revealed in all things, even in words, objects, and places. These are known as sacramentals, which are not to be confused with sacraments. Sacramentals are instituted by the Church; the sacraments are instituted by Christ.

Sacramentals provide grace that encourages Catholics to do good works, help diminish any venial sins they may have committed, and generally protect the soul. When Catholics practice "popular devotions," they are expressing ardor for God. According to the ruling of Vatican II, "Devotions should be so drawn up that they harmonize with the liturgical seasons, accord with the sacred liturgy, are in some fashion derived from it and lead the people to it, since the liturgy by its very nature far surpasses any of them" (from *Sacrosanctum Concilium*—Constitution on the Sacred Liturgy—Article 13).

Many devotional practices center on the Mass services held inside the church, and several of the objects that enhance these services are considered sacramentals. Understanding the role these objects play in the Church helps bring a greater understanding of the services themselves and what they mean to those who practice them.

The altar is the centerpiece of Catholic worship. It consists of a raised, tabular surface, on which the celebration of the Eucharist is performed during a Catholic Mass (see Number 50). Catholic laity may have small private altars at home to be used for prayer, but the sacrifice of the Mass cannot be performed there. Church altars must be consecrated.

The altar has a number of physical attributes, but the most essential is the tabernacle (from the Latin word for "tent"). This is where the consecrated communion bread is kept. Because of the holiness of what they contain—the Body of Christ—tabernacles are kept locked.

Holy water is an important sacramental that dates back to A.D. 400. Priests bless water to make it holy; in turn, the holy water may be used for blessings, to remove venial sins, and to purify worshipers in the presence of the Lord. That is why it is always found in a font at the entrance to churches (except during Lent in some places). When parishioners enter the church, they dip a finger in the water and make the sign of the cross over their person.

The most important use of holy water is in the sacrament of Baptism. When a baby or an adult is baptized, a little holy water is sprinkled over its forehead to symbolize the washing away of original sin.

Christian churches have burned **incense** since ancient times. The deep pungent smell lends an aura of solemnity to church services. The smoke drifting toward Heaven is a symbol of the direction of prayer toward God. Incense is most often used at solemn occasions such as funerals and processions.

Commonly used in pagan rituals, **candles** have also been a part of the ceremony and celebration of Christ from the early days of the Catholic Church. The candle is an outward and visible sign that reading the Gospel brings joy and light to the church.

Many Catholic ceremonies involve the use of candles—indeed, the rites of all but one sacrament (Penance) require them. It is forbidden to say the Mass without the presence of burning candles. The "tabernacle light" kept lit before the presence of Christ is in honor of His being among us at Mass. This tradition began in the 1200s and was made Church law in the 1600s.

Churches make use of many different candles. There are altar candles, which must be made of beeswax and should be white (in the ancient world, it was believed that bees were virginal, and using their wax would reflect the attributes of the Blessed Virgin Mary). The color of the candles changes to yellow during Holy Week.

Small votive candles, which are powerful symbols of prayer, are placed in front of statues of saints. To pray for a favor or to be remembered to Mary or Jesus, parishioners pay a small token to light one of these candles and place it before the statue of the saint being petitioned.

The tolling of **bells** has long been associated with churches and church service. The Catholic Church adopted bells as an essential part of church services sometime during the eighth century A.D. The great bells in the tower are used to announce the hour of services. In addition, a smaller bell placed on the epistle side of the altar is rung at the Sanctus, during a High Mass, to signal the adoration of the consecration of the bread and wine.

Confessionals weren't introduced until 1565. In the early days of the Church, the sacrament of Penance—asking for absolution for sins committed—was a public ritual reserved for very serious sins, such as murder. The sinner made a public apology and received a heavy penance.

In the Middle Ages, Irish monks instituted the idea of private confession, between a priest and the confessor, which usually took place before the altar. Later, this idea spread through the rest of the Church. In 1565, St. Carlo Borromeo, a powerful cardinal, designed a box that held a chair to provide anonymity for the confessor. By the 1600s, the Church had mandated that all confessions be heard this way.

Today, private confession always takes place in a confessional box, usually a wooden structure with a compartment for the priest and two additional compartments on either side for the confessors (so the priest can listen to one confession while the other confessor is getting ready).

⬿ 49 ⬿

THE MEANING OF SACRAMENT

The concept of sacramentality is essential to the Catholic faith. Sacramentality is the principle that says everything in creation—people, movements, places, the environment, and the cosmos itself—can reveal God. Under this principle, the division between sacred and secular is erased: Everything is sacred, because all comes from the Lord. (For more about sacramentals and sacramentality, see Number 48.) Beyond sacramentality as a general concept, Catholicism recognizes seven specific sacraments that confer grace.

The seven sacraments, which, in the Church's view, have been given to us by Christ, are Baptism, Confirmation, the Eucharist, Penance, the Anointing of the Sick, Holy Orders, and Matrimony. Through the sacraments of Baptism and Confirmation, Catholics are entitled to take part in the Church's liturgy (or worship). Ordination is a sacramental bond that ties the priest and the liturgical action to the ministry of the Apostles and to Christ. Priests, who are ordained ministers, are there to serve the baptized by administering the sacraments and through celebrating other parts of the liturgy, such as Mass.

Baptism, Confirmation, and the Eucharist are called the Sacraments of Christian Initiation. In the early days of the Church, catechumens (or initiates to the faith) received them all at once. These sacraments are the cornerstones of Catholic life: "The faithful are born anew by Baptism, strengthened by Confirmation and in the Eucharist receive the food of eternal life" (Paul VI, AAS 63 [1971] 657). Penance and the Anointing of the Sick are known as the Sacraments of Healing, and Matrimony and Holy Orders are sometimes called the Sacraments of Commitment.

In addition to grace, the sacraments of Baptism, Confirmation, and Holy Orders confer a sacramental character, or "seal," upon the believers. The indelible sign of each of these sacraments remains as a promise of divine protection and a call or vocation to worship and service, and it helps the believer to be permanently disposed to receiving grace.

Through grace, the sacraments are also instruments of salvation. The sacraments are efficacious, because Christ and the Holy Spirit are the ones at work through the sacraments, and they stand as reminders and guarantees of eternal life in God.

Catholics believe that the sacraments, or the rites of the Catholic Church, are the sacred base of a good Catholic lifestyle. The sacraments also remind us that we carry Jesus with us through our daily lives.

∞ 50 ∞

TRANSUBSTANTIATION AND THE CELEBRATION OF THE EUCHARIST

The Catholic belief in God as a real, living presence is best exemplified in the Eucharist, another of the mysteries fundamental to the Catholic faith. The word *Eucharist* originates from the Greek words *eukharistos* (thankful) and *kharis* (grace or favor). As the third Sacrament of Initiation, the Eucharist is absolutely central to the Church's liturgy, for it is concerned with the Body of Christ, the source of the Church's entire spiritual good.

Celebration of the Eucharist, the Mass, in what is known as the Eucharistic assembly, is the centerpiece of Catholic worship. During this ceremony, the assembly partakes of bread and wine that, through consecration by a priest, are converted into the Mystical Body and Blood of Christ. Consecration takes place when the priest says the words, "This is my body, broken for you. This is my blood." A special wafer, unleavened bread made only of wheat flour and water, is used. The wine must be a natural wine made of grapes. Drops of water are mixed with the wine to symbolize Christ's humanity and divinity combined.

In the Catholic Church, only the priest may consecrate the bread and the wine of the Eucharist. The priest has the power by virtue of his ordination to make Christ present and to reveal His death and Resurrection. The Church itself passes this power on to a priest through the sacrament of Holy Orders, linking Church, priest, and laity in the Eucharistic sacrament. In the modern Catholic Church, deacons may hold the cup during consecration, and deacons or lay ministers may distribute communion.

Ordinarily, only confirmed Catholics may take communion in a Catholic Church. However, under special conditions, individual non-Catholic Christians may share in Eucharist with Catholics.

The process through which the bread and wine are converted is known as "transubstantiation." Through transubstantiation, the Catholic Church teaches that in a mystical way, the sacramental bread and wine literally become the Body and Blood of Christ. In sharing this sacrament, the entire Catholic community is united in communion with Christ. For this reason, the Mass is also known as the Holy Communion. (Other names for this sacrament include Lord's Supper, the Breaking of the Bread, Holy Sacrifice, Sacrifice of Praise, Holy and Divine Liturgy, and Most Blessed Sacrament.)

The Church teaches that the Eucharist is both the outward sign of and the cause of all Catholics' communion in the divine life and with each other. It is the central means by which Christ sanctifies the world, and by which Catholics worship Christ, God the Father, and God the Holy Spirit.

Bread and wine are the outward signs of the Eucharist because, at the

Last Supper, they are what Jesus blessed and gave to His disciples in His memory. As Jesus proclaimed, the wine He offered was His blood; the bread, His body. Bread and wine are symbols that hearken back to the Old Testament. These things represented the first fruits of the Earth and were used as sacrificial offerings in the temple. Unleavened bread commemorates the bread that the Israelites ate on the eve of their flight from Egypt and the manna that fell for them in the desert. The wine is reminiscent of the Cup of Blessing at the end of a Passover meal.

By leaving this sacrament of His own Body and Blood, Jesus was able to remain forever with His disciples. The continual practice of this tradition is a memorial to Jesus and His life, death, and Resurrection; it will be performed until His final coming. The Book of Acts of the Apostles recounts how the Apostles preached and taught their followers and then broke bread with them at their homes. Christians usually met to break bread on Sunday, the first day of the week, the day of Jesus' Resurrection. That tradition evolved into Sunday Mass, which today is the center of the Church's liturgical and community life.

∞ 51 ∞

BAPTISM: SPIRITUAL PURIFICATION AND REBIRTH

The Church teaches that Baptism is the portal to spiritual life and the gateway to other sacraments. It is a sacrament of purification and rebirth.

Through Baptism, Catholics become members of the Church to share in its mission.

The practice of baptism, the cleansing away of sin, began when John the Baptist baptized Jesus at the River Jordan. Converts to early Christianity underwent baptism as a symbolic cleansing of sins and a public demonstration of their faith. Not until the Middle Ages, however, did infant baptism become an accepted practice. As previously mentioned in the discussion of limbo (Number 44), infant mortality was high, and many parents feared that their unbaptized babies would not get into Heaven.

The word *baptism,* from the Greek *baptizein,* means to "plunge" or "immerse." The immersion into the water is symbolic of death and rebirth: The baptized person "dies" in the water and is reborn in Christ, just as Christ Himself died on the cross and was resurrected. The waters of Baptism have a cleansing effect, as the soul of the baptized person is washed and renewed by the Holy Spirit. Baptism is also associated with spiritual enlightenment.

Many stories in the Old Testament seem to prefigure Baptism, including the story of the Great Flood, when the water drowned the wicked; the crossing of the Red Sea, which freed the Israelites from bondage; and the crossing of the River Jordan into the Promised Land. In the New Testament, as mentioned above, Jesus Himself is baptized before beginning His mission. After Pentecost, the Apostles began to baptize new converts to the faith.

In the early Church, Baptism was part of the Sacraments of Initiation, which also involved Proclamation of the Word, acceptance of the Gospel, profession of faith, the outpouring of the Holy Spirit through Confirmation, and admission to Eucharistic Communion.

Today, Baptism is traditionally administered shortly after birth, but the Church also practices adult Baptism. Adult Baptism hearkens back to the days of the early Church, with the Rite of Christian Initiation for Adults (RCIA). As catechumens, adults prepare to receive the sacraments of Baptism, Confirmation, and Communion. They learn about the mystery of salvation, the virtues, and the life of faith, liturgy, and charity.

Ordinarily, bishops, priests, and deacons are the only ones who have the privilege to baptize. However, the Church considers Baptism so crucial to salvation that anyone, even an unbaptized person, can perform the Baptismal ceremony in an emergency—as long as the minister of Baptism follows the ceremony and has the right intentions.

Baptism confers a number of benefits upon the recipient, including the forgiveness of all sins, personal as well as inherited (due to original sin), inclusion in the Church, and membership in the common priesthood of all believers. Baptism also provides justification that allows the sinner to believe in, hope in, and love God; to live under the influence of the Holy Spirit; and to grow in the moral virtues. Finally, it leaves an indelible spiritual mark that demonstrates the baptized person's dedication to Christ.

52

The elements of the Baptismal ceremony

There are special liturgies and preparations for adults who convert and are baptized in the Catholic faith (see Number 90). However, the majority of Catholics are baptized as infants, a tradition that dates back to the early days of the Church. Because Baptism washes away sin, and the Church taught that it was necessary for salvation, parents and Church ministers were reluctant to wait for children to grow up before being baptized. On the positive side, there seemed no reason to wait to give the baby the gift of purity and grace. Thus the practice of infant baptism became accepted.

Babies are too young to have faith because they lack perception. However, the Church teaches that they can receive grace because all sacraments work *ex opere operato*—by virtue of their own action.

First the priest pronounces prayers of exorcism over the baby. Then he anoints the child with the oil of the catechumens (a special oil blessed by the bishop and used during the baptism ceremony). Next, on the baby's behalf, the parents and godparents renounce Satan and all his pomp and works (the sins and vanities of the world). Then, the adults say the Creed, pronouncing their own faith and faith on behalf of the infant, whom they promise to raise in the Church.

Next, the priest carries out the actual baptism by pouring water over the head of the infant and saying, "I baptize thee in the name of the

Father, and of the Son, and of the Holy Spirit." Through the pouring of the water the infant is reborn again with and in Christ.

The final actions include the anointing with chrism, the sign of Christianity, in which the anointed shares in the essential powers of Christ. (Chrism is a mixture of oil of olives and balsam, blessed by a bishop and used for administering certain sacraments or performing certain ecclesiastical functions.) The infant is adorned in a snowy white garment, a symbol of purity of the infant's soul, full of grace and free from sin. The white garment identifies each baptized infant with the shining garment in which Christ appeared during the Transfiguration. Finally, the priest passes a lit candle to the godparents and says a prayer that the newly baptized may be faithful to Christ unto his last day.

All the newly baptized need help to grow in the faith, which is why every baptized person has a godfather and a godmother. These individuals, who act as sponsors, must be firm believers. For every infant who is baptized, the parents choose godparents, who must be Catholic. The understanding is that godparents are there to help the parents in acting as spiritual guides and as role models. They are also expected to make sure the child gets a Christian education if the parents are lax about it. Godparents are meant to help the newly baptized grow in the faith, and they play an important role throughout the child's life.

Baptism is usually a day of celebration for the infant's family. Extended family and friends gather for the ceremony, which is usually held in conjunction with Sunday Mass.

∽ 53 ∽

Confirmation: fully receiving the Holy Spirit

Confirmation is the second Sacrament of Christian Initiation, and it has an important relationship to the sacrament of Baptism. The Church teaches that Confirmation completes Baptism because it tightens the bonds between the person receiving the sacrament and the Church. At Confirmation, the confirmed receive the Holy Spirit more fully, and "they are, as true witnesses of Christ, more strictly obliged to spread and defend the faith by word and deed" (*Lumen Gentium* 11, OC, Introduction 2).

After Pentecost, the Apostles were filled with the Holy Spirit and began to proclaim the mighty works of God. Those who accepted the Gospel and were baptized also received the Holy Spirit through what was referred to as the "laying on of hands." The laying on of hands led to the ceremony of Confirmation, which carries the grace of Pentecost through the Church. The confirmed were again anointed with perfumed oil (chrism), in imitation of Christ, who was anointed by God with the Holy Spirit.

Anointing with oil signifies and imprints a spiritual seal; it is a sign of consecration. Those who are anointed take a greater part in the mission of Jesus Christ and the fullness of the Holy Spirit. The seal of the Holy Spirit is on them, symbolizing an affiliation or belonging. The Church teaches that the seal of the Holy Spirit marks the Christian's total belonging to Christ, his enrollment in his service forever, and the promise of divine protection.

Today, most Catholic children are confirmed in their early high school years. (According to canon 891 of the 2000 National Conference of Catholic Bishops, Confirmation should be performed before children are age sixteen.)

In the Catholic Church, the Confirmation liturgy contains the renewal of baptismal promises and the profession of faith. Adults who are baptized usually receive Confirmation and participate in the Eucharist immediately. When confirming adults who have just been baptized, the bishop extends his hands over the whole group and invokes the Holy Spirit: "Send your Holy Spirit upon them to be their helper and guide." Next is the laying on of hands, the anointing of the forehead with chrism, and the words, "Be sealed with the Gift of the Holy Spirit." The sign of peace concludes the sacrament.

Before Confirmation, most people study the actions, mission, and gifts of the Holy Spirit (see Number 54). They gain an awareness that they belong not just to their parish but also to the universal church. Those who are about to be confirmed receive the sacrament of Penance and seek the spiritual guidance of a sponsor.

In the Catholic Church, the bishop usually ministers Confirmation, though he may also delegate it to priests. If someone is in danger of death, any priest may confer Confirmation.

The sacrament of Confirmation affects a Catholic in many ways. First, it increases baptismal grace, unites the recipient more firmly to Christ, and perfects his or her bond with the Church. It also increases the gifts of the Holy Spirit and brings the strength of the Holy Spirit to spread and defend the faith, to openly admit to, and to never be ashamed of being a Christian. Finally, like Baptism, it imprints an indelible spiritual mark on the recipient. This gives the confirmed person the power and the authority to profess faith in Christ to all who would hear.

∞ 54 ∞

THE GIFTS AND FRUITS OF THE HOLY SPIRIT

As previously noted, Confirmation is a reaffirmation of Baptism and baptismal grace. There is an outpouring of the Holy Spirit, as there is in Baptism. Confirmation completes initiation into the Church community. It is a sacrament of maturity, in that it strengthens the recipient to grow into his faith, to live it more fully and actively, and to never be ashamed to tell the world that he believes in the Gospel of Christ.

As a milestone in a Catholic's life, Confirmation dovetails nicely with a child's coming of age. It reaffirms the maturation process and the development of faith. The lessons leading up to Confirmation teach that the grace of Confirmation can strengthen recipients to resist any peer pressure that might lead them into sin. On the other hand, Confirmation catechesis teaches that a devout Catholic should never bully or pressure another into accepting his beliefs. As a sacrament of maturity, Confirmation requires and supports good judgment. At Confirmation, the Gifts of the Holy Spirit help to strengthen a Catholic's faith. These Gifts include:

Knowledge, wisdom, and understanding, which help Catholics to set
  their store by God, virtue, and prayer; to gain insight into the mysteries of faith; and to be able to explain their faith to others

Counsel in helping Catholics follow God's plan for their lives by
  making correct decisions

Fortitude to be faithful Christians even when it's difficult to do so

Piety, which inspires Catholics to love God and to worship Him
  through prayer, liturgy, good works, and ministries

Fear of the Lord, which means an awareness of the evil of sin and a
  sense of awe and wonder at God's greatness

The confirmed also receive the fruits of the Holy Spirit, manifest in
relationships with God and with others.

Charity: Love for God and fellow human beings

Joy: Happiness that comes from living a Christian life

Peace: Inner calm despite life's difficulties and trials

Kindness: Concern and empathy for others

Goodness: Living justly as an example for all

Continence: Restraint and moderation in the pursuit of pleasure

Mildness: Gentleness in words and demeanor

Fidelity: Loyalty to God, spouse, family, and friends

Long-suffering: Patience in enduring suffering of any nature

Modesty: Respect for one's own body and the bodies of others in dress,
  conversation, and behavior

Chastity: Control over sexual impulses and a respectful attitude toward others

⤨ 55 ⤪

RECONCILIATION: CONTRITION, REPARATION, AND FORGIVENESS

Reconciliation, also called penance or confession (because it involves disclosing one's sins to a priest), is a sacrament of Healing, along with the sacrament of Anointing of the Sick. Reconciliation is also the sacrament of conversion and forgiveness: It is a turning point for one who has strayed from God through sin, and it confers pardon and peace through the priest's absolution, which is part of the sacrament. Through God's love, a sinner is brought back to union with the Father.

When Christians are baptized, they are cleansed of all sins. However, the Church recognizes that the Kingdom of God on Earth is a work in progress, and Christians cannot always avoid temptation or know how to make the right choices. The sacrament of Reconciliation allows the faithful to turn away from their sins and toward God in a constant cycle of penance and renewal.

This practice has been present since the earliest days of the Church. In times of persecution, some people denied Christ in order to save themselves from death by torture. Catholic communities accepted the apostates' public reconciliation, following in the spirit of Christ's message of forgiveness and compassion. Later, confessions became private.

Paul wrote, "Those who approach the sacrament of Penance obtain pardon from God's mercy for the offense committed against Him and are, at the same time, reconciled with the Church, which they have wounded" (from the Catechism).

The Church teaches that only God can forgive sin. However, it also believes that God gave to the Apostles and their successors the power to forgive sins in His name, in what the Church refers to as the Ministry of Reconciliation.

Because they have received Holy Orders, bishops and priests have the power to forgive all sins. The Church teaches that confessors should know what is to be expected in Christian behavior, have an understanding of human affairs, and treat the sinner with the respect every human being deserves. Confession is a sensitive matter; therefore, priests are bound to keep secret anything they are told in confession, and they cannot make use of any knowledge they gain of penitents' lives.

Penance requires the sinner to feel contrition or sorrow for the sin committed and to make a firm resolution not to sin again. Penance also requires confession, which helps the sinner take full responsibility for the sin. The last component of the sacrament of Penance is satisfaction: The sinner must do something to make amends for his or her sins.

In its tradition, the Church recognizes many ways in which the faithful do this. Common acts performed as Penance include:

- Fasting, prayer, and almsgiving
- Praying for the intercession of the saints
- Making peace with others
- Changing one's ways and making a commitment to being a better person
- Showing concern for the spiritual welfare of others
- Practicing and defending justice
- Shedding tears of repentance
- Examining one's conscience
- Taking spiritual direction
- Accepting suffering
- Enduring persecution for the sake of righteousness
- Following Jesus Christ
- Receiving First Reconciliation and First Communion
- Performing acts of devotion, such as reading Sacred Scriptures, praying the Liturgy of the Hours, and saying the Our Father
- Observing the seasons and days of Penance in the liturgical year, including Lent and Fridays

The Sacrament of Reconciliation allows the faithful to experience an interior conversion. Sinners feel sorrowful and repentant, and they respond to grace, which turns them back toward God. During His own lifetime, Jesus taught us to forgive when He shared His meals with sinners, and forgiveness and reconciliation remain essential themes of the Church to this day.

56

Receiving First Communion and First Reconciliation

The Church realizes that children struggle to grow up and live in the world and, just like adults, they need the grace and benefits of the sacrament of the Eucharist. First Holy Communion is a significant milestone in the life of a young Catholic. Church writings have said that it is appropriate for Catholics to make their First Communion once they have "reached the use of reason," that is, once they are around seven years old. By that point, they know, or can figure out, the difference between right and wrong. Cognitively, they are able to learn quite a bit through stories and examples; developmentally, they can be cooperative and attentive during the course of a school day. As members of their families and of their school communities, they are also ready to partake of communion, and to be full-fledged members of the faith community.

Age seven is the ideal age to learn about the Eucharist and to understand lessons from the life of Christ. Children of this age are usually eager to please and cooperate. If they have been raised with love and attention, they can naturally show care and concern for others.

At this point, children also begin to think logically about life's actual experiences. They are interested in learning beliefs, myths, and moral rules (although they tend to take their lessons quite literally).

In preparation for First Communion, many Catechism studies for the early grades focus on stories and parables from the life of Christ.

Teachers also use stories and examples to teach the Beatitudes, along with the importance of getting along with and caring for others, having a pure and joyful attitude, and helping the less fortunate.

Rather than focusing on sin, catechetical teaching before First Communion wisely concentrates on the positives instead. It uses stories and examples to teach children how to be holier and more Christlike, in preparation for receiving the body of Christ.

Once they reach this developmental stage and have had the proper Catechism preparation, children are ready to receive the Eucharist in the fullest sense of the word. As they trust and love their parents, they can trust and love Jesus. They can accept that God is their Father in Heaven and that Jesus is present in the Eucharist, though they may not grasp the full implications of it all. They can understand how to live like Christ in the world, which means treating others with love, apologizing when wrong, helping the less fortunate, and so on.

A child's First Holy Communion is usually a joyful occasion. For the actual Church ceremony on this special day, children often don new suits or new white dresses. Usually, the First Communion is a public, communal ceremony. Family members and good friends are present to share in the liturgy and the celebration afterward.

Today, Catholic children normally also have their First Reconciliation around the age of seven or eight. In fact, First Confession was once a prerequisite for First Communion, but that is no longer necessarily the case. Most theologians acknowledge that most children do not have serious sins to take care of before receiving the Eucharist. Some parishes let the parents decide whether or not the children are ready. The criterion is that the child knows the difference between more serious and less serious sins.

The benefit of confession at a young age is that it establishes the habit of using the sacrament of Penance. (The Church requires regular confession. It is mandatory for all Catholics to confess at least once a year as part of the Easter season.) Whatever the age, however, receiving the sacrament of Penance demands a full examination of conscience preceding confession, a willingness to be completely open and honest during confession, true contrition, and an agreement to do penance and to amend one's ways.

Penance can be therapeutic in the truest sense for children just as it can be for teens and adults. This sacrament can bring healing to a person's life by helping him or her regain a clear conscience, make amends, get some guidance, and start again.

First Reconciliation can be a memorable experience in a child's life. Cognitively, children are able to learn the commandments and what is expected of them. They are also concerned with what is just and fair. However, it is in later years that, alongside the markers and milestones of adolescence and adulthood, Reconciliation can be significant both in helping with problems and pressures and in serving as an instrument of personal growth.

57

ANOINTING OF THE SICK:

STRENGTHENING THOSE TIRED BY ILLNESS

The Anointing of the Sick is the second sacrament of Healing. In the New Testament, Jesus showed great compassion for the sick and performed many healings in His lifetime. In curing sufferers, He often asked them to believe; in healing, He used outward signs such as the laying on of hands and getting people to bathe themselves. The sick often tried simply to touch Him, believing they could be healed that way. Through His sufferings, Jesus joined in the sufferings of the sick.

In the early days of the Church, Anointing of the Sick was not focused on the dying, as it later came to be. In the Book of Acts of the Apostles, Peter and the other Apostles anoint the sick. They act on the specific directive of Jesus, who tells them to heal in His name. Thus, healing and the laying on of hands were part of the Apostles' mission. "In my name . . . they will lay hands on the sick, and they will recover" (Mark 16:17–18). Today, the Church strives to care for the sick and make sure they are remembered in prayers. In addition, the Church offers them a special sacrament, the Anointing of the Sick. The purpose of this sacrament is to strengthen those who are tired by illness. There is testimony that this sacrament has existed since the earliest days of the Church, when the sick were anointed with blessed oil. As time went on, that anointing with oil was reserved for people who were close to death, and the sacrament came to be called Extreme Unction. However, this rite has always contained an intercession and prayer that the sick person recovers, as long as it would be helpful to his or her salvation.

The Church teaches that anyone who seems to be in danger of death from sickness or old age is eligible for and should receive the sacrament of the Anointing of the Sick. When an illness worsens, the sacrament may be received again. If someone who has been gravely ill receives the sacrament, then recovers, he or she can receive it again during another grave illness. Those about to undergo a serious operation, as well as elderly people who have become much more frail, can receive this sacrament, too.

Only priests are allowed to administer the sacrament of the Anointing of the Sick. The Church treats the performance of this sacrament as a communal liturgy no matter where it is celebrated, even in a home or a hospital room. It can be administered to a particular patient or to a group of sick people. The Church celebrates the Anointing of the Sick as part of the Eucharist, preceding it by the sacrament of Penance, if circumstances allow.

The anointing with oil and prayers confer several benefits upon an ailing believer, including strength provided through the grace of the Holy Spirit; closer union with the suffering of Christ; a contribution to the holiness of the Church; and preparation for the journey to everlasting life.

58

Finding meaning in sickness and suffering

In the New Testament, Christ healed many people who were acknowledged to be hopeless cases. He did this as a demonstration of divine power and also out of compassion. However, He did not heal everyone. The Church teaches that sickness is related to the sinful state of mankind, but it is not directly related to an individual's sins. It is not meant to be a punishment. People must accept their sickness and find meaning in their suffering as they find their own path to God.

The Church also recognizes, however, that sickness and suffering are serious problems for humanity. While illness does lead some people to turn against God, it can also help the faithful realize what is important in life and turn them toward God.

People who have been religious or spiritual throughout their lives tend to become more observant as they age. As Catholics grow older, death, an important transition, looms before them, and their thoughts turn to the afterlife. As such, the final anointing given to a Catholic on his or her deathbed is a fitting and useful milestone.

Of late, however, the Church has emphasized the sacrament's healing role. As discussed above, the dying are not the only ones encouraged to take advantage of this sacrament.

The Church teaches that the sacrament of Anointing of the Sick has actual properties for healing the body because there is a connection between body and soul. Elderly people often suffer from depression and weariness, and so may be more focused on what is to come than on their present existence. Sick people fall into despair, and may give up all hope, because they are caught up in their own suffering. Because the sacrament of Anointing of the Sick brings hope and comfort, improvements in psychological states may also contribute to improvements in the physical states. But even those people who do not recover, or who recover only to relapse again, draw strength and meaning from the sacrament. The sacrament can help these individuals rise above their illness, refocus their life on the essentials, draw closer to God through the power of the Holy Spirit, and be more long-suffering and hopeful.

For the frail, elderly, and those with serious or terminal illnesses, death is an undeniable inevitability and a significant transition they must face sooner rather than later. And for many who develop cancer or suffer a heart attack in midlife, serious illness is a reminder of their mortality. Illness becomes a milestone in these people's lives; it is a transition with major psychological and emotional consequences. The grace of the sacrament of Anointing of the Sick can help people with serious illnesses integrate what is happening to them into their spiritual lives to attain growth and understanding.

But the meaning that can be derived from sickness extends beyond just the individual who is sick. The Church teaches that all Catholics can be living, breathing sacraments of healing as they help those who need emotional, mental, or physical healing. Possibilities for this are endless, and Catholics are encouraged to bring healing to others in a variety of ways, including visiting the sick and the dying; volunteering in hospices or hospitals; helping the physically, mentally, or emotionally ailing; assisting the homeless and indigent; and reaching out to patients who are afflicted with AIDS, cancer, and other terminal illnesses.

∽ 59 ∽

HOLY ORDERS: BECOMING A MINISTER OF THE GOSPEL AND THE SACRAMENTS

The Church teaches that two kinds of priesthood share in the high priesthood of Christ. One is the priesthood of the faithful, made up of ordinary people who participate in the priestly character of the Church through Baptism and their own vocations. The Church teaches that everyone shares in the priestly character of Christ as they share in His life, suffering, and death.

The second priesthood is the ministerial, or hierarchical, priesthood of bishops and priests. Christ develops and leads His Church through the ministerial priesthood. Through the sacrament of Holy Orders, members of the ministerial priesthood may act in place of Christ and in the name of the Church.

Holy Orders is a sacrament conferred on men, by which they carry on the apostolic tradition as ministers of the Gospel and the sacraments. The term *order* comes from the Latin *ordinatio*, which means incorporation into an *ordo,* an established civil or governing body. The Church is made up of three orders: episcopate (bishops), presbyterate (priests), and deaconate (deacons). To join one of these orders, initiates participate in a liturgy of induction, which varies depending upon the order.

As discussed in Part 2, of the three orders—bishops, priests, and deacons—the episcopal order, composed of bishops, holds the highest place in the Church. Each bishop is a link in the apostolic line, an unbroken succession going back to the earliest days of the Church. At the apex of the sacred ministry, they receive the full powers of the sacrament of Holy Orders: to sanctify, teach, and rule. Bishops are also the ones who become pontiffs and pastors. The episcopal order is collegial, which means that bishops work together in the consecration of a new bishop, and each bishop is responsible for the apostolic mission of the whole Church.

Priests are consecrated to help bishops in the work of the Church. They preach the Gospel, take care of the faithful, and celebrate the holy liturgies. They carry out their ministries in communication with and in service to their bishops, whom they promise to love and obey. All priests are members of a priestly college, or presbyterium.

Deacons are at the lowest end of the clerical hierarchy. They assume Holy Orders through a special imprint or seal that marks them as ministers, deacons, or servants. Deacons are generally attached to the bishop who ordained them. They assist him in celebrating the Eucharist, distributing Holy Communion, assisting at and blessing marriages, proclaiming the Gospel and preaching, conducting funerals, and working in charitable ministries. Deacons may be married.

A bishop performs the sacrament of Holy Orders, laying hands on a candidate and reciting a specific consecratory prayer. In the Catholic Church there are accompanying rituals, such as the presentation, instruction, and examination of the candidate. Celibacy is one of the conditions for receiving Holy Orders for all but permanent deacons.

If initiates are to be ordained as bishops or priests, they are anointed with holy chrism, a sign of the special anointing of the Holy Spirit. New bishops also receive the books of the Gospels along with the ring, miter, and crosier as symbols of apostolic mission. Priests receive the paten and chalice, through which they make offerings for the Church to God. Deacons receive the books of the Gospels, to proclaim the Gospel of Christ.

∽ 60 ∽

MATRIMONY: LIFELONG PARTNERSHIP IN GOD'S LOVE

Through the Catholic sacrament of Matrimony, a man and woman commit themselves to a lifelong partnership. Married couples receive God's grace to perfect their love, to strengthen their unity, and to help each other attain holiness. Catholic marriage is a vocation (a calling), and it requires the married couple to accept certain obligations toward each other, their children, and the community. The marriage bond is established by God and can never be dissolved. It requires total fidelity from the spouses and the openness to bearing children and educating them in the faith.

Catholicism adopted the sacrament of Matrimony from the Jewish tradition. The Old Testament states that human beings were made in the image and likeness of God, and that man and woman were made for each other; through marriage, they become one. Furthermore, the Church teaches that because God created human beings out of love, and calls them to love, it is fitting that the union of man and woman should be a sacrament. The spouses' mutual love mirrors love of God; their children, who are their own creations, are also part of God's creation.

Whereas an ordained minister, priest, or bishop confers the other sacraments in most cases, marriage is unique. The spouses actually confer the sacrament of Matrimony upon each other when they express their consent to marry before the Church.

The marriage ceremony of two Catholics normally takes place at Mass, in memory of the paschal mystery and the way Christ bound Himself permanently to the Church, His beloved bride. Numerous prayers ask God's grace and blessing on the couple, and the Holy Spirit infuses the couple with unending love and strength for fidelity.

The exchange of consent between the spouses is an indispensable element of the marriage ceremony. Marriage without consent, performed with coercion or threats, is invalid. The presence of the priest or bishop and of other witnesses testifies to the fact that marriage is part of the Church. As a sacrament, Matrimony is part of the Church's liturgy, and therefore it needs to be celebrated publicly.

If a Catholic person wishes to marry outside the faith, he or she must obtain permission from an ecclesiastical authority for the marriage to be valid in the eyes of the Church. The dispensation is based on the couple's acknowledgment of two things: the goals and behaviors of marriage, and the Catholic person's requirement of preserving his or her own faith and ensuring that the children are baptized and raised in the Church.

Some dioceses have programs that help interfaith couples fulfill their obligations, encourage what they hold in common, and increase respect for their differences. The Church believes that the Catholic partner's love, practice of family virtues, and prayer can help the other partner to convert.

The Church understands that the evil in the world makes marriage difficult. Jealousy, power struggles, and conflicts can lead to bitterness and separation. However, Jesus taught that marriage is indissoluble: "Therefore, what God has joined together, no human being must separate" (Matthew 19:6). Through the sacrament of Matrimony, the Church teaches that Jesus gives the strength and grace to live the real meaning of marriage. As Paul wrote in exhortation, "Husbands, love your wives, even as Christ loved the church and handed Himself over for her to sanctify her" (Ephesians 5:25–26).

∞ 61 ∞

WHAT HAS SHAPED THE CHURCH'S MODERN VIEW ON MARRIAGE?

Matrimony was the last of the sacraments to be established, around the year 1200, which is quite late in the history of the Church. The purposes of marriage within the Church have changed and have been challenged since earliest times.

In the early days of the Church, married couples who converted to Christianity did not have to be remarried in the Church; their marriage was considered valid. The Church also recognized civil ceremonies between two Christians as valid for creating a Christian marriage. The Church did not require the blessing of a priest or any other liturgical trappings.

During the Middle Ages, when other European tribes overran the Roman Empire, a conflict arose between Roman civil law and European law and custom regarding marriage. European law held that marriage was a contract; that the couple owed each other sexual rights to procreate; and that witnesses and a formal ceremony were required. Parents who arranged marriages for their children to increase their power and property wanted marriages to be public contracts. However, Roman law held that only the couple's vows to each other were important and that they could be taken in private. A whole series of popes declared on the side of Roman law, ruling that marriage was the result of a couple's mutual consent and nothing else. No witnesses were required, and no contract needed to be signed.

This privacy led to problems. Parents who arranged marriages in what they held to be the best interest of themselves and their children were still being thwarted. There were abuses as well. Jealous or greedy people could prevent someone's marrying by claiming they had already wed someone else in private, and no one could dispute these false charges.

In the twelfth century, at the Second Lateran Council, theologians declared Matrimony to be a sacrament, and this declaration was later upheld by the Councils of Lyons and Florence. The Church decided upon three essential statements on matrimony:

1. The grace of the sacrament is to assist the couple to grow in holiness and perform their married duties.
2. To reflect Christ's fidelity to His Church, marriage must be indissoluble.
3. The real ministers of the sacrament of Matrimony are the marriage partners themselves; they confer the sacrament on each other.

The more public form of marriage did not receive a formal introduction until the Council of Trent decided in 1563 to consider valid only those marriages that had been celebrated before a priest and two witnesses. Later, in 1917, the Code of Canon Law went further. Marriage gained status as a contracted, legal proceeding that was understood to be the exchange of rights to sexual intercourse with the purpose of begetting children, which according to the Church was the primary purpose of marriage.

Vatican II softened this strict view of marriage by redefining it as a sharing of life between two human beings who love each other. The begetting of children is seen as a natural development from this sharing.

Modern Catholics face many social issues regarding marriage: high divorce rates, couples living together outside of marriage, fertility technologies that allow single women to have children, and other stresses on the traditional family unit. The Church sees these practices as problematic and has come to appreciate even more the love and faithfulness in an authentic marriage. Today, the Church places less emphasis on marriage as a contract, on whether each member of the couple is a baptized Catholic, and on how children fit into the picture.

The Church understands that valid marriages sometimes become untenable for one or both partners. However, given the indissoluble nature of the bond of marriage, a Catholic cannot remarry while the former spouse is still living. A person who does so commits a grave sin and cannot receive the Eucharist or enter fully into the life of the Church. If a person lives a chaste life while his or her former spouse remains alive, he or she remains a member of the Church in good standing.

That said, spouses seeking to dissolve a difficult marriage have been able to do so through the process of annulment. If one party forced or tricked the other into marriage, did not want to or was unable to consummate the marriage, or never intended to have children, the other partner can have the marriage declared invalid. More recently, some marriages have been annulled on the grounds that a "community of love" could not be entered into or sustained.

Ultimately, Matrimony remains a celebration of the transcendent mystery of a couple's love and faithfulness. The Church supports those virtues through pre- and postmarital counseling and education, helping couples grow, develop, and sustain their affection and fidelity through the years of their married lives.

Part 4

SCRIPTURE
INTERPRETATION

CATHOLICS BELIEVE THAT ONE OF THE WAYS GOD COMMUNICATES with His people is through the Bible, which is divided into the Old Testament (revealed to the Hebrews) and the New Testament (the Gospels and other Christian works). The Church has specific methods for interpreting the Scriptures and stresses the importance of tradition and papal authority in scriptural studies.

The Church believes that God does not leave the faithful to figure out His mysteries on their own. The Bible reveals God's wisdom and teachings and is an essential part of divine revelation. Catholic doctrine holds that neither the Gospels nor the Bible's other books are self-explanatory. To understand these texts and see the truths they contain, people need the guidance of the Church. The highest authority in interpreting the Scriptures is the pope.

THE COMPILATION OF THE BIBLE

The Catholic Bible is a collection of poems, history, literature, and letters. The Old Testament, drawn from the Jewish tradition, is composed of Hebrew and Aramaic writings. The Torah (the first five books of what became the Hebrew Bible) guided Jews' devotional life. The version the early Christians used was the Septuagint, the Hebrew Bible translated into Greek by Jewish scholars in Alexandria, Egypt, around A.D. 250. By the end of the fourth century, St. Jerome made another translation from Hebrew into Latin, known as the Latin Vulgate. Later editions of the Vulgate continued to be used for the next thousand years.

The writings eventually compiled into the New Testament were composed in the second half of the first century A.D., and well into the next century, as the new Church was growing and expanding through the Mediterranean region. These writings included the Gospels—Matthew, Mark, Luke, and John—as well as a number of epistles and other writings in Greek. At the Council of Trent, the gathered bishops reaffirmed which of these devotional writings would be accepted as sacred. The Church believes the Holy Spirit guided the bishops at the Council of Trent (1545–1563) as they chose the writings that would be deemed sacred. The complete list is called the Canon of Scripture.

Through the centuries, it has been the practice of the Church to provide newly converted nations with vernacular versions of the Scriptures.

In the first 500 years of the Church's history, translations of the sacred writings were common. In its second millennium, the Church began to fear heresies and misinterpretation of the book and was concerned about the spiritual welfare of untutored people who might read the translations, so the Bible became far less frequently available to laypeople.

In 1564, however, Pope Pius IV began to allow vernacular editions of the Bible to be studied among learned men. Many later clergy had doubts about the laity having access to translations of the Bible, but in the evangelical age, when the Church was sending missions to all corners of the globe, the Bible was widely translated.

The Catholic Church understands that any vernacular Bible is an imperfect translation of God's original message. Words and phrases in both Greek and Hebrew can have several meanings. A scholar educated in these languages must go back to the earliest versions available to make a fuller interpretation.

∞ 63 ∞

THE OLD TESTAMENT

Jesus was a Jew, and many of His earliest followers were also Jewish. They saw their belief in Christ's death and Resurrection as a continuation of Jewish tradition. Through their forefathers Abraham and Noah, the Jews had established a covenant with God. Part of this covenant was the promise of a Messiah who would save humankind. Jesus' birth and death fulfilled the message of the prophets and established a New Covenant between God and humanity. The ancient writings that foretold a Messiah and gave the history of the people are thus part of the Christian tradition.

At the time the Bible was compiled, letters were laboriously copied by hand onto parchment scrolls. At the Council of Trent, the Church pinpointed forty-six Old Testament books that must be considered "as sacred and canonical," seven more than are included in most Protestant Bibles. Both Protestants and Catholics refer to the extra books contained in the Catholic Bible as Apocryphal (from the word "apocrypha," meaning "hidden") or Deuterocanonical (meaning "second canon"). In addition, the Catholic Bible contains portions of the books of Esther and Daniel that do not appear in the Hebrew Bible.

The first five books of the Old Testament, known as the Pentateuch (Greek for "five books"), recount the stories of Creation, the covenant between God and Noah, and the law delivered by God to Moses. Following the Pentateuch are the historical books. These end with the books of Tobias, Judith, and Esther, which relate personal history. Following the historical books are the books on law, arranged by the Council of Trent to reflect their order of writing. Then come the books of the Prophets: The first four are known as the Major Prophets, and the last twelve are Minor Prophets, arranged in chronological order. Finally, the Psalms and Proverbs compose the works simply called the Writings.

Most Christians, including Catholics, read the Old Testament in the light of Christ crucified and risen, but the Old Testament retains its own intrinsic value as revelation reaffirmed by the Jesus Himself, who quoted frequently from the books included in the Old Testament.

∞64∞

THE NEW TESTAMENT

During the course of Christianity's first four centuries, the development of the New Testament occurred through a long and laborious process of collecting, reviewing, and accepting or rejecting material. The books of the New Testament continued to be debated and scrutinized until 397 A.D., when, at the Council of Carthage, another canon was released and the twenty-seven books we now know as the New Testament were agreed upon.

Early Church fathers divided the New Testament into the Gospels and the Acts—works that occurred during Jesus' and the Apostles' lifetimes—and the later didactic writings. The New Testament begins with the four Gospels, which hold a unique place in the Church, as they are the heart of all the Scriptures and the center of the liturgy. Next comes the Acts of the Apostles, followed by the didactic writings—a series of letters from Paul to scattered Christian groups struggling against a hostile world. The Pauline Epistles include Romans, Corinthians 1 and 2, Galatians, Ephesians, Philippians, Colossians, Thessalonians 1and 2, Timothy 1 and 2, Titus, Philemon, and Hebrews. The later Catholic Epistles, the Apostolic Letters of James, Peter 1 and 2, John 1, 2, and 3, and Jude, are additional letters on Church life. The New Testament closes with the Apocalyptic Book of Revelation. Many of the writings were probably completed by the year 125 A.D., although some may have been written considerably later.

Catholics believe the New Testament must be read in light of the Old. Early Christian catechesis made constant use of the Old Testament. When contemporary Church scholars seek biblical interpretation, they may consult additional Hebrew, Aramaic, and Greek writings, including earlier versions of the Bible and works such as the Dead Sea Scrolls or the Nag Hammadi.

In 1947, Bedouin shepherds searching for a lost goat in the Judean desert came upon some jars in a cave. Archaeologists subsequently excavated the Qumran ruin of structures between cliffs near the caves and the Dead Sea, which led to the discovery of thousands of scrolls and fragments scattered in eleven caves. Written during the late Second Temple Period—the time when Jesus lived—the Dead Sea Scrolls predate other surviving scripture manuscripts by almost 1,000 years.

In 1945, an Arab peasant unexpectedly uncovered a collection of more than fifty texts at Nag Hammadi, Egypt. Among other writings, these texts contained Gnostic Gospels, such as those of Thomas and Philip, written before a single version of orthodox Christianity had been defined. Gnosticism, which was eventually deemed heresy, focused more on divine revelation as an ongoing force, rather than the development of one standardized, static creed. Among other things, the Gnostics believed in the power of individual revelation and experience, as well as the dual—masculine and feminine—nature of the divine.

Over the past fifty-plus years, the Dead Sea Scrolls and the Nag Hammadi manuscripts have sparked public interest. Because of these recent discoveries, the New Testament is undergoing a re-evaluation.

THE CHURCH'S TEACHING ON INFALLIBILITY

According to the Catechism of the Catholic Church, "In order that the full and living Gospel might always be preserved in the Church the Apostles left bishops as their successors. They gave them 'their own position of teaching authority.'" Indeed, "the apostolic preaching, which is expressed in a special way in the inspired books, was to be preserved in a continuous line of succession until the end of time."

Through this continuous line of succession, the Church was able to assert its authority and to establish a system of beliefs and traditions that trace back to the early days of Christianity and the time of the Holy Spirit's descent. As a consequence of this succession, a tradition developed whereby some of the laws issued by the pope were believed to be infallible, which is the reason why the Church was able to establish the books that truly belonged in the Bible. (Catholics, therefore, are expected to accept the Church's interpretation of God's Word as inspired by the Holy Spirit.)

The dogma of papal infallibility was not formally promulgated until Vatican I (1869–1870). As the visible head of the Church, the pope is infallible in his teachings on matters of religion and morality. However, the Church does recognize the fact that popes can and do make mistakes in their actions. As such, teaching must now be "received" by the whole Church to be seen as truly infallible. This is actually a modified definition of papal infallibility, devised by the 1965 Vatican II Council.

This evolving concept of infallibility has eased ecumenical discussions with other religions. For example, Pope John Paul II, in his overtures to the Eastern Orthodox Church, has acknowledged that the Church erred and contributed to the Great Schism that split the Catholic Church.

Not only the pope is viewed as infallible; the Bible itself, being God's Truth, is seen as equally infallible. The Catholic Church considers all of the Scriptures to be God's sacred Word dictated through the Holy Spirit and, thus, they are entirely true and correct. The Church does, however, acknowledge that the Bible sometimes contains contradictory verses and advice. Consequently, Church fathers believe that each passage must be studied in the context in which it was originally written and in light of the overall message of God's love. (See Number 67.)

∞ 66 ∞

HOW DO CATHOLICS INTERPRET SCRIPTURE?

Catholics do not interpret the Scriptures as the full message of God but as a component—the written message that must be interpreted together with the oral traditions passed down by the Apostles. Through the example of their lives and work, their preaching after Jesus' death, and the institutions they established, the Apostles continued to pass on the Gospel. Today's Church leaders, the bishops, are direct successors to the Apostles, passing down through the ages the wisdom learned in earlier times.

Church tradition and acquired belief is just as important as words written in the Bible. Alone, the Bible is not sufficient for understanding the full Christian message. Catholics must also listen to the teaching of the Church to make sense of the Scriptures. The Catholic Church looks behind the words for the intent of the Great Author.

Church tradition includes a long, rich heritage of biblical interpretation. The Holy Spirit speaks to Church fathers to help them interpret the Bible, but they can only understand within the bounds of current human knowledge. Giving an authentic interpretation of the Word of God, whether in its written form or as tradition, is entrusted to the Church, a living, teaching office instituted by Jesus Christ. In the Church, the authority of interpretation rests with the bishops and the pope. The role of ordinary Catholics is to accept and understand these teachings.

According to the Catholic Church, the Bible does not contain all of God's truth. The role of the Church is to reveal God's truth throughout the ages, and so the Church itself is an instrument to proclaim the Word of God. It is a witness and guardian of revelation and thus more qualified than are individuals to determine the meaning of the Divine Word.

In its insistence on balancing Scripture and tradition, the Catholic Church continued a Jewish tradition of oral interpretation, or elaboration, of the law. In making Peter the rock on which He built His Church, Jesus set in motion a hierarchy. The pope or Bishop of Rome is the successor to Peter. Each of these Church leaders is seen as having power and access to the Holy Spirit. The Catholic Church continues this tradition of apostolic succession to the present day.

Catholics share the conviction that the Bible is the Word of God. The Holy Spirit inspired and spoke through the writers of Scripture. Although they were ordinary men who acquired knowledge through ordinary channels, they spoke with divine authority. The Bible is a constant source of revelation as Church fathers return to it to reinterpret God's Word for the modern age. It is also a constant mystery, as human understanding does not extend to the full power of God's message.

The Bible's spiritual and historical context

In the Scriptures, God spoke to human beings in a way they could understand. To interpret Scriptures correctly, the reader must be aware of what the human authors truly wanted to affirm and what God wanted to reveal. Bishops, priests, and laypeople educated in theology have spent untold hours puzzling over the meaning of the Bible's words and stories.

The Bible is a work of history and literature, switching from genealogy and historical accounts to poetry and parables. It is an ancient text that has been copied by scribes over and over again. Furthermore, it is a work in translation from ancient Hebrew, Aramaic, and Greek, languages spoken thousands of years ago.

The Bible reflects a history of a certain people, the tribes of Israel in the Old Testament, followed by a history of the early Christian Church in the New Testament. Catholic scholars and historians agree on the historicity of the Gospel tradition, but they differ about the extent to which each Gospel story can be affirmed as historical. The Church accepts that many writings were influenced by the historical context of the time, and they might have much less relevance for succeeding generations.

The stories of the history of the Israelites and Abraham's descendants are one of the ways that God shows us His presence in the world. God communicates Himself to human beings gradually, with His words and His deeds. These include the great flood, the choice of Abraham to lead God's people, and the Exodus from slavery in Egypt. The divine plan of revelation begins in the Old Testament, but the plan is not fully revealed until the New Testament. In the Hebrew stories, God is preparing human beings for the person and mission of the incarnate Word, Jesus Christ.

Keeping all this in mind is important. Readers must remember that while there may be a literal meaning to many Bible stories and passages, there is nearly always a spiritual meaning as well. In fact, a rich reading of Scriptures should encompass four senses:

1. **The literal sense:** The literal meaning of the passage as a story or instruction.

2. **The allegorical sense:** A more profound understanding of events in the Old Testament can be achieved by understanding their parallels in the New Testament.

3. **The moral sense:** The Scripture is written for our instruction and ought to lead us to act justly.

4. **The anagogical sense:** We can view today's events in terms of their eternal significance. (*Anagogical* comes from the Greek *anagoge*, "leading.")

68

SYMBOLISM AND METAPHOR IN THE BIBLE

Catholic interpretations accept that the Bible is full of symbols and metaphors that are not meant to be taken literally. As science and human knowledge progress, the Church has been able to reconcile the stories of the Bible with current knowledge. By contrast, some Protestant communities take the Bible literally and believe, for example, that human history began 6,000 years ago with Creation.

Catholic scholars point out the myth and legend involved in some biblical stories, which may have been written down after being passed on orally for generations. The Creation myth is one example of using symbols to show God's plan for the world. The Church does not insist that it is pure history. Instead, it is willing to accept the theory of evolution and scientific theories that attempt to explain the origin of the Earth. The Creation myth is seen as a metaphor for God's master plan for the world. God made everything that exists, and everything He made is good. Through evolution, He allows higher forms of beings to emerge from lower, less complex forms, and His pinnacle of creation is humankind.

The rainbow is a powerful symbol of God's covenant with Noah and his successors. The crossing of the Red Sea is a sign of Christ's victory and also of Christian baptism. A journey in the wilderness is a powerful metaphor for a spiritual search—Jesus performed such a journey, following the example of His forefather Moses and that of the prophets. Water is another a recurring symbol throughout the Bible—it washes away sin and symbolizes new life.

Catholics see the Bible as a literary work that was written by people who were speaking to their contemporaries. As a piece of literature, it contains imagery and storytelling that best illustrates the points the writer wanted to emphasize.

Like all literature, some books of the Bible are stronger than others. The Church regards some pieces as better written, and some as more filled with the power of the Holy Spirit than others. Theologians and writers both often hold up the Book of Job as a work of great literature. Some books, such as the Psalms and the Song of Songs, were written as poetry.

In the New Testament, the Gospel writers took great pains to tie Jesus' birth and the events of His life to the messianic predictions of the Old Testament. There are mystical parallels running through biblical stories, such as the forty days of Noah's journey and Jesus' forty days in the wilderness, and Jonah's three days in the whale and Christ's three days in Hell. Likewise, Jesus' new commandment, to love one another, is an extension of the ten given to the Jewish people by Moses.

Stories emphasize the way Jesus lived His message. For example, He is frequently shown working with the poor, the sick, and the social outcasts. Symbols such as the tree and the cross, the vine and the vineyard, the bread and the wine appear repeatedly in the texts to illustrate Jesus' covenant with the world. The parables—Jesus' anecdotes illustrating man's relationship with God—are powerful stories within the Gospels.

∽∾ 69 ∽∾

WHY THE CHURCH ONCE DISCOURAGED THE LAITY FROM READING SCRIPTURE—AND HOW THAT HAS CHANGED

Catholics believe study increases their sense of spiritual reality and the Scriptures can grow with the one who reads them. The Scriptures—including both the Old and the New Testament—should be an integral component of each Catholic's daily life. Although Catholic laity was once discouraged from reading the Bible, the importance of studying the Holy Book both in church and at home has been emphasized since Vatican II.

In the past, Church officials worried that evil might come from the laity studying the Scriptures because they would be in danger of misinterpreting biblical passages. Therefore, officials decreed scripture may only be interpreted by those ordained in the Church. Today, however, reading and understanding the Bible does not seem the daunting task it may once have been. The Church has recently noted growing enthusiasm about and interest in the Bible among the Catholic laity, who form study groups and gather informally to read and discuss the Scriptures.

Today, Catholics put great value in catechesis—an education in the faith—of children, young people, and adults. This includes especially the teaching of Christian doctrine and Bible study, as well as an awareness of Church interpretation and Church history. Catholic schools begin the education process with religion and family life classes. But Christian catechesis continues with adult Bible study, individual devotions and study, and the messages Catholics receive during Mass from their priests.

The Church believes that access to the Sacred Scriptures ought to be freely available to the faithful, wherever they live. It exhorts all the Christian faithful to learn "the surpassing knowledge of Jesus Christ" by reading the Bible often. Time and again, the Bible is a wellspring to which Catholics return for support, comfort, guidance, and food for the soul.

Still, Catholicism is not a "religion of the book." It is the religion of the Word of God, a living word that requires a vibrant tradition of interpretation by bishops and priests who instruct believers. At the same time, the Holy Spirit must be at work to open human beings' minds with understanding.

Part 5

PRACTICES
AND CUSTOMS

*T*HE CATHOLIC FAITH IS ONE DEEPLY STEEPED IN RITUAL AND tradition. Catholic practices and customs have evolved through the centuries through both formal decree by Church hierarchy and also through more informal development of rituals in the faith community itself.

Liturgy incorporates the formalized expressions, or rites, of public worship in many religions, and Catholicism has certainly developed its own liturgical ensemble. The Catholic Church teaches that those who participate in the liturgy are sanctified through it. The word *liturgy* descends from a Greek word that means "public duty," because liturgies are always conducted in a public setting. There are dozens of individual prayers that Catholics can draw on for every occasion and every detailed expression of faith and belief. But a few special types of prayers and practices, such as the Stations of the Cross and the Rosary, are highly devotional and symbolic in nature. These prayers are so elaborate, they are more like religious ceremonies or rites.

∽ 70 ∽

WORSHIPING AS A FAMILY

The family is the lifeblood and central unit of any Catholic parish. Indeed, the metaphor of family informs the entire structure of the Catholic Church. The family is an inviolable unit, one that gives great strength, comfort, and support in faith. A happy, healthy family leads to a happy, healthy life in general, so it is no coincidence that the Church considers the beginning of a family—Matrimony—to be so significant that is one of the seven sacraments.

The bonds of prayer tie a Catholic family together. Prayer brings holiness into the family and creates a ritualistic setting in which the family can unite in their common wishes and their faith. Parents introduce their children to prayers at a young age, and children grow up with a deep connection to prayer as a form of communication with their family and with God.

Grace before every meal is one common way that families bring God into their daily life. Food means comfort and sustenance. It is important to remember that it doesn't get to the table by itself. Parents provide and cook it. And God made the world from which the food springs. Thanking God is a good way to remind children not to take life for granted.

Many children are also taught to say a simple prayer before going to bed. This simple ritual of saying a bedtime prayer helps them calm down, forms a lovely bond with their parents, and fosters a long-lasting habit. Most important, it sets the stage for the development of faith as children grow older. Here is a sample bedtime prayer that many Catholic parents teach their young ones:

Matthew, Mark, Luke, and John,
Bless the bed that I lie on.
Four angels round my bed,
Two at the foot, and two at the head.

A family is also strengthened by its weekly adherence to Sunday worship. Attending Mass as a family unit is enriching. Praying and worshiping together during the liturgy spreads warmth that can't be denied. It raises everyone up and helps them to feel a little better about themselves. When children are older, partaking in the Eucharistic celebration is ennobling. The children are now soldiers of Christ and well on their way to becoming full-fledged members of the congregation.

Once introduced to simple devotional habits, a Catholic child will probably go to a Catholic school or Confraternity of Christian Doctrine (CCD) classes to learn their catechism properly and receive more disciplined Catholic teachings. During CCD classes, children receive an age-appropriate introduction to Bible stories. This gives them a taste of the great mysteries at the heart of Catholicism as well as instruction in catechism to help them begin their journey to becoming Catholic adults with a firm grasp on Catholic beliefs.

Ultimately, however, it is the parents who set the educational stage. By teaching children about prayer and Scripture, and making them parts of daily life, parents give their children an exemplary model for personal help and meditation for their whole lives.

∞ 71 ∞

RELIANCE ON A FAITH COMMUNITY

Catholics are communal people. They feel a need to be part of a bigger community and to receive challenging feedback from others with similar ideals. As expressed in Ephesians 4:4, there is "one body and one Spirit," just as "you were also called to the one hope of your call." In a spiritual sense, Catholics want support and company on their journey to God. Many Catholics enjoy the enriching experience of belonging to a faith community because of the interaction and the relationships they form there among people with common interests and beliefs.

The parish is the epicenter of each Catholic community. Here, you have people seeking God together in prayer and Catholic devotions. But there is also a growing movement toward more casual "faith communities," small gatherings at church socials or even at specially built centers (usually attached to a chapel or church) where people come together for discussion and prayer. These are more informal groups that, in a way, represent a beautiful tradition that dates back to the early Christian gatherings, when people met in private homes to practice their faith in secret.

For some, a faith community might be at a monastery; for others, it might be a prayer group. College students can find a spiritual home at a Newman Center on their college campus. Intended to serve the spiritual needs of Catholic students on campus, Newman Centers are named after the inspiring nineteenth-century English cardinal John Henry Newman. Now a worldwide movement, the Newman Apostolate originated in 1893 at the University of Pennsylvania, when a few students decided to organize in order to take action spiritually, intellectually, and socially. In a broader sense, a Catholic high school is a faith community because each student is surrounded by others who share a common Catholic upbringing.

Spiritual centers allow individuals a greater degree of participation in and understanding of their faith while reinforcing their sense of community. In a group setting, prayers become much more meaningful and also more natural, as people share their devotion with their friends.

∽∽ 72 ∽∽

STRIVING TO ACHIEVE A PERFECT STATE OF PRAYER

The Catholic Church deeply believes in the power of prayer to establish and uphold a very powerful spiritual relationship between God and human beings in Christ. Some Catholics simply call this "keeping company with God." The Catholic Catechism refers to it as a covenant relationship. As with everything else in the Church, the wellspring for this prayer is Christ made man, which is the Creator's ultimate act of love.

The revelation, or call to prayer, occurs first in the Old Testament and then is fortified in the New Testament. What's more, the style and mood of prayer changes from the Old Testament to the New Testament. The Old Testament is full of prayers of lamentation. In the New Testament, there are many prayers of petition and hope in the risen Christ.

Catholics strive to achieve a perfect state of prayer. Devotion (or deep belief), concentration, acknowledgment of dependence on God, a sense of gratitude to the Almighty, and attitudes of worship and praise are all elements that foster this perfect state of prayer. The example set before them is what the Church calls Jesus' "filial prayer"—his state of prayer when addressing His Father as well as the example of His life and sacrifice. The Church says that filial prayer, which is characterized by solitude, is the perfect model of prayer in the New Testament.

Key prayers of the Catholic Church include the following:

Our Father
Hail Mary
Glory Be
Apostles' Creed
The Rosary (a cycle of prayers that includes various combinations of those mentioned above, plus the Hail Holy Queen prayer)

(The wording of the Our Father prayer appears below; see Number 73 for the beginning of the Apostles' Creed. For the wordings of the other prayers mentioned above, visit *www.catholicdoors.com*.)

The Our Father is the fundamental prayer of the Catholic Church. Jesus Himself taught it to the Apostles, and it is considered a summary of the most important teachings in the Gospels. Catholics everywhere recite this prayer during the course of every Mass. In fact, this prayer, along with the Hail Mary, is the most common prayer Catholics say, among the thousands of other prayers available to them.

Our Father

Our Father who art in Heaven,
hallowed be thy name.
Thy kingdom come.
Thy will be done on Earth, as it is in Heaven.
Give us this day our daily bread,
and forgive us our trespasses,
as we forgive those who trespass against us,
and lead us not into temptation,
but deliver us from evil.
For the kingdom, the power, and the glory are yours, now and forever.

Though simple in its wording, the message of the Our Father is extremely powerful.

WHY DO CATHOLICS RELY ON THE SAINTS?

Catholics believe that human beings can be brought to a greater common awareness with God through the power of certain intercessors venerated by the Catholic Church. An angel, saint, holy person, or a priest can plead a believer's cause to God or, in other words, be a mediator between the believer and the Lord.

Mediation is a process that bridges the divide between the human and the divine. The saints, especially the Virgin Mary, take their spiritual power from Christ, the ultimate mediator, and can intercede with God to confer His grace on humans.

Saints are the spiritual leaders and role models of the Catholic community, those who lived a life of great piety and sacrifice and set a shining example of pure and immaculate spirits. The first saints were martyrs—those who died for their faith. These martyrs were inspiring and the faithful lavished devotion on them. In the days of the early Church, Christians would gather on the anniversaries of these saints' deaths to honor them. When persecution ended, there was an outpouring of love and honor, complete with immense tombs and special liturgies. The liturgical calendar was deluged with a feast day for each saint.

Devotion to the saints, long a cherished Catholic tradition, seems to have waned in recent years. The Scripture does not really dwell on the mystical bond with the saints in any depth. Yet, devotion to the saints can be a powerful aid to living a Catholic life in a troubled world, and Catholics are certainly expected to believe in the "communion of saints," who are with God in Heaven but still in communion with the followers on Earth through a common faith.

This belief is upheld in the Apostles' Creed, which states, "I believe in the Holy Spirit; the holy Catholic Church; the communion of saints." It is a resource and a community worth tapping. The saints can be called on to intercede with God on behalf of the faithful. (At Vatican II, the Church confirmed its teaching that Catholics should pray to the saints for intercession.) Catholics also can receive saintly guidance from these heroes and heroines of faith for their virtues of compassion, forgiveness, honesty, justice, patience, and wisdom.

Many of the saints were inspired writers. Today, Catholics seek out the words and works of such saints as St. Ignatius Loyola, St. Teresa of Ávila, St. Thérèse of Lisieux, and St. Clare, who—among others—help enrich understanding of God.

∞ 74 ∞

DEVOTION TO MARY THROUGH THE AGES

The Blessed Virgin Mary, the Mother of God, is one of the most venerated saints and important figures in Catholic liturgy. The Church has proclaimed five Marian dogmas (or truths), which devout believers uphold. These dogmas state that Mary is the Mother of God; that Mary is a perpetual virgin; that she was born by Immaculate Conception (conceived without original sin); that she was assumed into Heaven and did not suffer mortal decay; and that she is the Mother of the Church.

Mary embodies the great maternal impulses of kindliness and wisdom. As such, Mary is venerated around the world. And yet very little is known about her actual life. What we do know mostly comes from canonical Scriptures, especially the Gospels.

In the Gospels, Mark, Luke, and John all take a very different approach to Mary's role in the life and works of Jesus Christ. (The fourth Gospel, the Gospel of Matthew, is fairly similar to the Gospel of Luke.) The differences among their portrayals of Mary have implications both for how the Church understands her and on the Marian devotions practiced by believers. Many Catholics favor the images of Mary from the Gospel of Luke, which describes the Annunciation and includes a passage that extols Mary's virtues.

The Gospel of Luke shows Mary to be pious and obedient to God as it describes the birth of Jesus, the homage of the shepherds, and the presentation in the Temple. For the most part, Mary seems to understand her role in the divine plan.

However, Mark and John sometimes portray Mary in a less positive light. Take the passage of Mark 3:20–35 as an example. In this passage, Jesus and His disciples are in a house near the Sea of Galilee, and a huge crowd has gathered outside. Jesus' family comes to take Him, for they fear for His sanity. They say: "He is beside Himself." When someone tells

Jesus, "Your mother and your brothers are outside, asking for you," He replies, "Here are my mother and my brothers. Whoever does the will of God is my brother, and sister, and mother." This passage may lead to the assumption that Mary was not one of the original disciples, and Mark never says that she ever became one.

The Gospel of John initially seems to show that Mary does not have full knowledge of the divine plan. However, at the end of this Gospel, we see the Virgin Mary at the foot of the cross with John himself, one of Jesus' disciples. Jesus says to His mother, "Woman, behold your son," and to John, "Son, behold your mother." The Church interprets this as Jesus giving His mother a spiritual role as mother of the disciples. This role of discipleship is viewed as giving rise to the great doctrines and devotions to Mary that later developed in the Church.

Devotions to Mary have waxed and waned over the history of the Church, depending on the mood of the times, the doctrinal approaches of theologians, and the viewpoints of the popes. In the East, devotions to Mary were very strong, and Marian legends and hymns in honor of her were popular. New churches were dedicated to Mary. Christians celebrated Marian feast days and sang hymns to the Virgin.

In the West, devotion to Mary wasn't widely practiced until the time of St. Ambrose (339–397 A.D.), who believed that Mary could not have been the Mother of God without physical and moral purity and affirmed her close relationship with the Church.

By the time of the Middle Ages, Byzantine Mariology began to have a great influence on the Church in Europe. Hymns like "Ave Maris Stella," in which Mary is likened to the Star of the Sea, were added to the Catholic devotional practices. The Catholic Church began to see Mary as radiant, pure, and above the angels, a woman who redeemed mankind from the curse of the original sin of another woman, Eve. Mary was venerated as the Ark of Salvation, the ladder by which sinners climb to Heaven.

In 1124, Eadmer, Precentor of Canterbury and a disciple of St. Anselm, produced the first manifesto on the doctrine of the Immaculate Conception, which held that Mary is free from original sin because she is the Mother of the Redeemer and Empress of the Universe.

The doctrine was slow to be accepted. St. Thomas Aquinas held that because Mary was conceived, she must have been born with original sin. More than a century later, however, John Duns Scotus convincingly argued that Mary was preserved from original sin in anticipation of the divine goodness of Christ. In 1476, Pope Sixtus IV approved the feast of the Immaculate Conception. The doctrine of the Assumption also began to grow in strength during the Middle Ages.

Toward the end of the Middle Ages, Marian devotions had become excessive and even superstitious. With the Reformation, the Protestants rejected excessive devotion to Mary, though they did not abandon the Marian doctrines altogether. Luther and Calvin believed in her perpetual virginity and the respect due to her as the mother of Christ. However, Calvin rejected Mary's vital role as an intercessor for all sinners, and Protestants gradually dropped devotions to Mary, whereas in the Catholic Church, devotions to Mary gained strength.

75

MODERN-DAY MARIAN DEVOTIONS

The Enlightenment, an era of rational thought and scientific reasoning, saw decline in the popularity of Marian devotions because they were viewed as emotional excesses left over from a bygone era. However, the Church keenly felt the effects of the Romantic era, with its interest in emotional and mystical states. In the nineteenth century, with the strong approval of the popes, devotions to Mary surged back into mainstream Catholicism. Pius IX (1846–1878) championed the cause of devotion to Mary as an antidote to liberal rationalism and proclaimed the dogma of the Immaculate Conception in 1854.

Understanding of Mary and her role in the Church continued to change and develop throughout the twentieth century. Pope Pius XII, who led the Church from 1939 to 1958, was a devotee of Our Lady of Fatima; he consecrated the world to the Immaculate Heart of Mary and defined the doctrine of the Assumption—that Mary, like her son, was assumed to Heaven, body and soul. Pius XII also proclaimed 1954 a Marian year, dedicated to celebrating the 100th anniversary of the dogma of the Immaculate Conception.

Just twelve years after the dogma of Assumption had been passed, the Second Vatican Council convened in Rome to discuss matters of Catholic doctrines and faith. In particular, some discussions examined Marian devotion.

The council concluded that Mary should be viewed as a fellow member of the Church, not as a semi-divine being. The council also concluded that Catholics should refer back to the Scriptures to understand Mary and her role in the Church. The Church fathers warned Catholics not to place belief in Mary's power of intercession over their belief in Jesus Christ as the one mediator between God and humans. All of Mary's ability to mediate rests on the power of Christ, and veneration of Mary must foster our relationship with Him. Christ is the one who gave Himself for humankind's redemption. Mary, giving herself to God's will throughout her life, is the model of a good Christian, but she does not have special powers. The Church refers to veneration paid to Mary as "hyperdulia" because of the difference in degree from other forms of veneration; it is higher than veneration of saints but lower than veneration accorded to God.

However, Vatican II adhered to the most benign interpretations of Mary's role in Christ's ministry. In addition to being the Mother of God and Mother of the Redeemer, Mary also "belongs to the offspring of Adam and is one with all human beings in their need for salvation." This is a position that relies most on the Gospels and the early teachings of the Church.

Furthermore, at the closing of the third session of Vatican II (of the four sessions held in total), Pope Paul VI declared Mary the Mother of the Church, the Church's model in faith, charity, and perfect union with Christ. The Church, like a mother, brings forth her children for Baptism. While Mary has reached perfection, Catholics should see the Church as working toward the example that Mary sets.

As the modern Church reassessed Mary's position, feminist theologians also redefined their understanding of women's roles in the Church in light of Mary's example. They argued that if Mary is mother and minister to the Apostles, a larger role in the ministry of the Church must belong to women. Many feminists rejected the view of Mary as submissive to God's will and argued that her love forms a cornerstone of the Church.

Pope John Paul II recently emphasized the beliefs that the Roman Catholic and Eastern Orthodox Church share regarding Mary to help make advances toward rebuilding the schism between the two. In particular, he stressed the belief in Mary's title as Mother of God and "knowledge that the mystery of Christ leads us to bless His mother." John Paul also mentioned the common history the Catholics and the Eastern Orthodox Church have in venerating images of the Virgin.

A remarkable number of appearances of Mary, many to children and young people, have happened in the last few hundred years. They include Lourdes, France, in the nineteenth century; those at Cova da Iria, Portugal, in 1917; and in Medjugorje, Yugoslavia, in the 1980s. Throughout the 1980s, appearances were documented in Ireland, Egypt, and Italy. Witnesses often say that when they saw Mary, she had a message—to seek peace, to build a community of faith, or to return to a more spiritual life. These appearances have strengthened Marian devotion in recent times.

Throughout the year, the Church celebrates several feast days in Mary's honor:

January 1: Solemnity of Mary, Mother of God

May 31: The Visitation of the Blessed Virgin Mary

July 1: Immaculate Heart of Mary

August 15: The Feast of the Assumption

August 22: Queenship of the Blessed Virgin Mary

September 8: Birth of the Blessed Virgin Mary

November 21: Presentation of the Blessed Virgin Mary

December 8: The Solemnity of the Immaculate Conception

76

WHY DON'T CATHOLICS EAT MEAT ON FRIDAYS?

While the basic core of beliefs has not changed since Revelation (the Word of God delivered by Jesus Christ), some Catholic practices have changed through the years. Within the tradition of the Church, some customs–such as the practice of weekly confession, for example–have been left behind. This is only natural, as the Catholic Church has adapted to the needs of its membership at different times.

Another custom that has changed over the years is the Catholic practice of abstaining from food at certain times. Traditionally, Catholics practiced various types of abstinence from food as a penance for sins, and therefore a kind of cleansing, particularly before holy days, although this habit is not practiced as often as it once was.

One form of abstinence involved having only one full meal per day. Another prescribed the avoidance of meat or meat-based products and flavorings. This practice was reserved for Fridays, in recognition of Good Friday, when Jesus died on the cross, and explains why in the past, Catholics typically always ate fish on Fridays. However, it is no longer necessary to abstain from meat on Fridays, although believers may do other forms of penance to commemorate Christ's suffering. (It is still common for Catholics to give up something they enjoy or to work toward a positive goal during Lent, for example, as a way of honoring Christ during that important season.) In the United States, many Catholics continue to avoid meat on the Fridays during Lent as well as on Ash Wednesday, which is the first day of Lent. (See Number 89 for more about Lent.)

Another component of this practice of abstaining from food involves preparation to receive the Eucharist. At one time, Catholics were required to fast prior to partaking of the Holy Communion (usually from midnight to the following morning, until the Sunday Mass). These lengthier fasts are no longer required, however. At present, Catholics usually abstain from eating one hour prior to communion. This means no food or drink, except for water. (People who are ill may reduce their fast to fifteen minutes.) In this case, abstaining from food is done out of reverence for the Body and Blood of Christ.

77

THE STATIONS OF THE CROSS:
RETRACING THE STAGES OF THE CRUCIFIXION

The Stations of the Cross is a veneration that originates from the story of the Crucifixion. The Gospels recount how Jesus Christ was sentenced by Pontius Pilate and taken to Golgotha, where He was put on the cross, and they tell how He died. His journey, also known as Via Dolorosa, is broken down into fourteen stations. Each one has a symbolic role that helps the faithful contemplate the Crucifixion. The stations commemorate the following events:

1. Jesus receives His sentence—death by crucifixion.
2. The soldiers hand Him the wooden cross, which He must carry.
3. Jesus falls (for the first time) while carrying His cross.
4. On His way, Jesus encounters the Virgin Mary.
5. Simon of Cyrene carries the cross for Jesus.
6. Veronica gives Jesus her veil so that He may wipe His face.
7. Jesus falls again.
8. Jesus encounters the women of Jerusalem, who weep for Him.
9. Jesus falls for the third time.
10. The soldiers strip Jesus' garments.
11. Jesus is nailed to the cross.
12. Jesus dies on the cross.

13. The soldiers take Jesus' body off the cross.
14. Jesus' body is laid in the tomb.

The practice of following the Stations of the Cross started during the Crusades, when pilgrims to the Holy Land visited Jerusalem and followed the Via Dolorosa to the Church of the Holy Sepulcher (the site of the tomb where Jesus was buried and rose from the dead). It wasn't until the eighteenth century that Stations of the Cross were introduced inside churches.

In modern Catholic churches, it has become customary to set up the Stations of the Cross around the building's inside walls, with each station represented by a picture or plaque. This way, when people walk up the outside aisle and down the other, they can visit all of the stations while saying the attendant prayers.

∞ 78 ∞

OBJECTS SERVE AS REMINDERS

Catholics pay particular attention to religious objects. Symbols of Christ's suffering, representations of the Blessed Virgin, and other religiously significant medals, pictures, and statues comprise another type of sacramental, which has a special place in both the church and the home. It's important to understand that Catholics do not worship these items but rather use them as reminders of Christ, Mary, and the saints.

The crucifix, one of the universal symbols of Catholicism, venerates Jesus' suffering on the cross. The plain cross—two pieces of wood, a smaller length set about a third of the way down on a longer length at right angles—did not appear until the fourth century A.D., at the end of the persecutions.

The crucifix, which is a cross with the body of Christ figured on it, did not appear until the fifth century. It was frequently decorated with jewels during the fifth and sixth centuries, and became a highly glorified symbol. Nowadays it is usually much plainer and simpler, and it can be fashioned from any wood or metal. The crucifix is a symbol of hope and power. It is worn by many as a sign of their religion and of rejoicing in their spirituality. Catholic families commonly hang crucifixes in their homes and crucifixes appear in all Catholic churches.

Devotional **images and statues** honor Mary, the Mother of Jesus, as well as many saints. Usually, each saint is represented by a specific characteristic or symbol. For instance, statues of St. Peter show him holding the keys to the Kingdom of Heaven, which symbolically represent Jesus entrusting Peter, who eventually became the first Bishop of Rome, with authority to govern the house of God—the Church (Matthew 16:19). Likewise, Mary is frequently pictured as the Madonna, given her religious significance as the Mother of Christ.

The saints are also venerated through **relics**. The word *relic* comes from the Latin *reliquiae,* or "remains." Relics are material objects left behind after a holy person has passed away. They include personal possessions, or even parts of the body of a departed saint. These objects help the faithful recall their union with the saints and inspire them to lead lives of prayer and service.

In earlier times, a relic of a patron saint might actually be embedded in the altar of a particular parish. Now they are usually kept in holy places or in very special churches in the Holy Land, in Rome, and in other centers of early Christianity.

Catholics wear **scapulars** to show devotion to Mary, the Mother of God. The scapular, two pieces of brown cord made from woolen cloth, has pictures of Mary at either end. The bands rest on the shoulder and the pictures lie on the breast and the back at an equal distance from the shoulder. This practice originated in the thirteenth century, when St. Simon Stock saw an apparition of Mary, who told him that all who wore the scapular would be saved from Hell, for on the Saturday after their deaths she would take them to Heaven.

Holy cards are not intrinsically holy objects, but once a priest blesses a holy card, it becomes efficacious. Holy cards are meant to be inspirational. They are often given out to commemorate someone who has died, participation in an event, or a pilgrimage. They may also be handed around as small gifts to mark religious occasions—for instance, during Baptism, First Communion, or Confirmation. A holy card may feature a picture of a saint on one side and a prayer on another; some holy cards include inspirational quotes or the Ten Commandments.

The Rosary and Novenas

Mary is first among the saints, and therefore the first choice for the faithful who ask the saints to intercede on their behalf. Many prayers of the medieval Church that address Mary directly still survive today. Catholics commonly ask Mary, who embodies compassion and mercy, to intercede for them in prayers for friends and family who are ill and in trouble.

The Rosary is a series of prayers and meditations that Catholics recite, which encourages them to express their devotion to Mary and to reflect on the important events, or mysteries, of Christ's life as experienced by her. The prayers are spoken while fingering rosary beads, which aids in meditation and the contemplation of the mysteries. The word *Rosary* itself means "crown of roses." According to tradition, each Hail Mary prayer is a rose and each Rosary is like a crown of roses that the person reciting the Rosary presents to Mary. Although less emphasized in the modern Church, it is still an important devotion for many Catholics.

The Rosary forms a circle and consists of two main sections. The first, smaller part of the Rosary hangs down from a larger, circular section. It is a strand with a single bead, a group of three beads, and another single bead, followed by a crucifix. On the two single beads, the devotee says the Our Father and Glory Be. On each of the three beads, the devotee prays a Hail Mary. On the crucifix, the devotee repeats the Apostle's Creed. This sequence is something like an introduction to the rest of the Rosary.

The second part forms the actual circle. On a full rosary, there are fifteen decades, or groups of ten beads. A bead in between each group separates each decade. On each of the ten beads, the devotee says a Hail Mary, and on the in-between beads, the Our Father and Glory Be. Each decade is dedicated to a particular mystery from Mary's life. (See Number 72 for the Our Father prayer, and *www.catholicdoors.com* for other prayers.)

More commonly, Catholics use smaller rosary beads with five decades, and recite prayers while reflecting on one set of mysteries. They then go around again for each of the other sets of mysteries. Each set of mysteries covers key moments in the New Testament, as follows:

1. **The Joyful Mysteries** are the Annunciation, the Visitation, the Nativity, the Presentation of Jesus in the Temple, and Jesus found in the Temple.

2. **The Sorrowful Mysteries** are the Agony in the Garden of Gethsemane, Scourging, Crowning with Thorns, Carrying of the Cross, and the Crucifixion.

3. **The Glorious Mysteries** are the Resurrection, Ascension, the Holy Spirit revealing itself, Mary taken into Heaven, and Mary crowned Queen of Heaven.

4. **The Light Mysteries**, which have been added by John Paul II, are Baptism of Jesus, Wedding Feast at Cana, Proclamation of the Coming of the Kingdom of God, the Transfiguration, and the Institution of the Eucharist.

It is said that St. Dominic, who lived in the thirteenth century, preached the importance of saying the Rosary daily because he believed it would protect Catholics from evil and sin. Originally, the faithful recounted 150 psalms, but because many of the faithful were illiterate and could not memorize all of them, they said 150 Our Fathers instead. Still later, the sequence of Our Fathers was replaced with Hail Marys.

Novenas are prayers, either private or public, that may have a sense of urgency because of the specific intention of the prayer—to pray for someone who is very sick or in trouble of some kind. The faithful can use any prayer to recite a novena, although saying the Rosary or particular prayers to one of the saints are often common choices. Derived from the Latin word *novenus*, meaning "nine each," in a novena, prayers are said for nine consecutive days to obtain special favors or to make a special petition. The nine-day cycle symbolizes the time between Christ's Ascension into Heaven and the coming of the Holy Spirit, when Mary and the disciples devoted their time to prayer, waiting for divine guidance and inspiration.

Though novenas don't have an official place in the liturgy of the Church, they are very popular. The choice of saint usually depends on the specific request. For example, a person might pray to St. Peregrine, the patron of cancer patients, for special intervention for a loved one suffering from that illness. People also pray to St. Jude for desperate situations and hopeless cases—anything from a runaway teenager to an out-of-work husband to a family member suffering from a mental disease.

One popular novena is the Divine Mercy Novena, handed on to us from a Polish saint, Faustina Kowalska, who died in 1938. She was canonized in 2000 because, during her life, she helped convey new forms of devotion to divine mercy.

Novenas are often associated with a special request for Mary's intercession, and The Immaculate Heart of Mary, a devotion that concentrates on the love she bore her son and the piercing of her heart at the Crucifixion, includes a popular novena prayer.

∽ 80 ∽

THE ELEMENTS OF THE CATHOLIC MASS

The Catholic belief in God as a real, living presence is best exemplified in the Eucharist, one of the mysteries fundamental to the Catholic faith. Celebration of the Eucharist—the Mass—is the centerpiece of Catholic worship.

The Mass incorporates the profession of faith (through the recitation of the Nicene Creed), reading of Scripture, and the sacrament of the Eucharist. The liturgy of Mass begins with the Last Supper; the Passion, Death, and Resurrection of Christ form its nucleus. The Mass is both a banquet and a memoriam of the Crucifixion.

The liturgy of Mass includes High Mass and Low Mass. The High Mass, which is much more intricate, is reserved for special feast days and is usually performed by a bishop or another venerated ecclesiast. It also requires the assistance of a deacon and the presence of a choir. A priest, attended by an altar server, generally performs the Low Mass, which is held daily. Sunday Mass, of course, has special significance, and the Church requires attendance of its members on this day.

During the Mass ceremony, the assembly partakes of bread and wine that, through consecration, are converted into the Mystical Body and Blood of Christ. As explained in Number 50, the process is known as "transubstantiation." Through transubstantiation, the bread and wine are literally changed into Christ's body and blood. In sharing this sacrament, the entire Catholic community is united in communion with Christ. For this reason, the Mass is also known as the Holy Communion.

The entire liturgy of the Mass, which consists of two parts, is structured around the Eucharist. The first part consists of the gathering or coming together of the faithful; the Liturgy of the Word, with readings from the Old and New Testaments (commonly, a passage from the Gospels); the exhortation of the priest to the people, which is known as the homily; and general prayers of intercession for the needs of the faithful.

The second part, the Liturgy of the Eucharist, includes the presentation of the bread and wine, or the Offertory, in which the bread and wine are brought to the altar; the consecration, which includes the Eucharistic prayer of thanksgiving and consecration, in which the priest asks the Father for the power of the Holy Spirit to turn the bread and wine into the Body and Blood of Christ; and finally, the communion. The Our Father and the Breaking of Bread precede the communion proper, whereby all the faithful partake of the Body and Blood of Christ.

The Church recommends that anyone who may do so should receive communion at Mass, because of the powers of Holy Communion, which include the following:

- It increases the Catholic's connection with Christ.
- It separates the faithful from sin by wiping away venial sins and protecting the Christian from future mortal sins.
- It draws the faithful closer to the Church, the mystical body of Christ.
- It commits the faithful to the poor.
- It promotes unity with all Christians.
- It is a celebration of the glory that is to come.

Because they are about to receive the body of Christ, Catholics are expected to prepare before communion, to examine their consciences, to confess their unworthiness, and to pray for the healing of their souls.

∞ 81 ∞

THE NICENE CREED: PROFESSING FAITH IN JESUS' HUMANITY *AND* DIVINITY

The Nicene Creed, handed down in part from the Council of Nicaea, states belief in the divinity and humanity of Jesus. Composed of twelve articles of faith, the Nicene Creed incorporates the most basic beliefs of

Catholicism. The authoritative wording has guided the Church for 1,600 years and forms the expression of faith that Catholics recite during Baptism as well as at the celebration of the Eucharist during every Mass.

The formulation of the Creed was a defining moment for the Church, and it came about through a reaction to the rising tide of a heresy called Arianism, which threatened the unity of the Christians in the fourth century by denying the divinity of Jesus Christ. To deal with the growing controversy, Emperor Constantine, the first Roman emperor to convert to Christianity, called a council of bishops to Nicaea.

The Nicaean Council, which met in 325 A.D., developed the Nicene Creed from the Apostles' Creed. Until the 1500s, the Apostles' Creed was believed to be a summary of the Apostles' faith, since it was neatly composed of twelve articles of faith, the same number as Jesus' chosen disciples. During the 1400s, though, historians discovered its true origin, as an adapted version of the old Roman Creed. (The Apostles' Creed remains the most important creed of most Protestant religions.)

The Nicaean Council refined the wording of the Apostles' Creed so that Jesus' divinity—in addition to His humanity—was plainly expressed and proclaimed. A second ecumenical council that convened in Constantinople in 381 A.D. approved and finalized the work of the first council, giving us what we now know as the Nicene Creed.

The full text of the Nicene Creed is as follows (bracketed text indicates original wording—small changes have been made in the modern text that Catholics now use):

We believe [I believe] in one God, the Father Almighty, maker of Heaven and Earth, and of all things visible and invisible. And in one Lord Jesus Christ, the only begotten Son of God, and born of the Father before all ages. [God of God] light of light, true God of true God. Begotten not made, consubstantial to the Father, by whom all things were made. Who for us men and for our salvation came down from Heaven. And was incarnate of the Holy Ghost and of the Virgin Mary and was made man; was crucified also for us under Pontius Pilate, suffered and was buried; and the third day rose again according to the Scriptures. And ascended into Heaven, sits at the right hand of the Father, and shall come again with glory to judge the living and the dead, of whose Kingdom there shall be no end. And [I believe] in the Holy Ghost, the Lord and Giver of life, who proceeds from the Father [and the Son], who together with the Father and the Son is to be adored and glorified, who spoke by the Prophets. And one holy, catholic, and apostolic Church. We confess [I confess] one baptism for the remission of sins. And we look for [I look for] the resurrection of the dead and the life of the world to come. Amen.

82

THE EVOLUTION OF THE LITURGY

The liturgy in its present form has been in development for more than 2,000 years. During the early days of the Church, the rites were not harmonized in any standard format. They were a fluid group of elements, often practiced with different customs according to local preference. It wasn't until the Council of Nicaea in 325 that the liturgy of worship started taking on a formalized order and shape.

Since then, the rites and customs of public worship have been fine-tuned, adapting to the changes of history and the modifications in Church canon law. The two councils that were especially significant in implementing official shifts in emphasis were the Council of Trent and the Second Vatican Council, commonly known as Vatican II.

The Council of Trent ruled that Christ is *actually* present in the sacrifice and celebration of the Eucharist. Furthermore, the council's decisions led to the publication of a missal that standardized the prayers and rites of the Mass.

In the middle of the twentieth century, Vatican II introduced several notable changes to the liturgy. Its most significant and controversial change was that vernacular (that is, the native language of the congregation) was allowed to be used in conducting the Mass. When reciting the Nicene Creed and other prayers, the congregation's native tongue ensures they fully understand and are able to relate to what they are saying. Although

Latin was dropped from most parts of the service, it has not been discarded completely. It remains one of the unifying features of the Church.

Other changes included moving the altar so that it faces the congregation; decreasing the number of prayers said during Mass; and encouraging parishioners to join in the singing (rather than listening to a choir).

During Vatican II, the Holy See also redirected emphasis to interior worship, reminding Catholics that they must celebrate Mass in a "right form of mind." This ruling was made in reaction to a misconception that observing the rituals is enough to get salvation. The Church wanted to impress upon the faithful that they needed to pair observance of the rituals with interior prayer to achieve a state of grace. As previously stated, within Catholicism, the Mass, or Eucharistic celebration, is the central liturgical service. But because of the sacramental nature of Catholicism, Catholics can worship through all things. So, for instance, the administration of the sacraments is also considered a great part of the liturgy of Catholicism, as are other formalized rituals.

In addition, the liturgy of the Church is attuned to the year, or seasons, as they pertain to Christ's life. Indeed, each day holds a special significance in the Church, although there are certain high points that take place in the course of a year. The most important is the Easter cycle, but a number of solemnities, feasts, and memorials also have special significance.

83

LITURGY OF THE WORD

As explained in Number 80, the Mass consists of two major sections. The Liturgy of the Word is the first part, but before it takes place, the Mass begins with greeting rites that prepare the assembly—as a community—to hear the Word of God and celebrate the Eucharistic sacrifice. First, there is the entrance antiphon, which is a few lines from a psalm sung or chanted by the congregation. Then there is a greeting period, which is followed by a penitential rite (a rite of blessing and sprinkling). Then, the congregation recites Gloria (Glory to God) and the opening prayer.

The Liturgy of the Word follows the introductory rites. The purpose of this section of the Mass is to proclaim God's Word to the assembly, as it is understood from Scripture. Here the Word of God is spoken, responded to, explained, embraced, and appealed to.

The First Reading is almost always taken from the Old Testament. The congregation follows the reading with a Responsorial Psalm. The Second Reading is an encouragement, taken from one of the epistles of the New Testament. At the Gospel Acclamation, the Alleluia, all members rise. The Gospel is the central reading of this part of the Mass.

When going to Mass, it is important to note that the liturgical calendar, in Sunday worship, follows a cycle that changes over a three-year period: Matthew is the primary Gospel in the first year, followed by Mark the following year and Luke the third year.

After reading the Gospel, the priest gives his homily, a short speech drawing relevance from the Gospel to daily life. There is a moment of silence, then the recitation of the Nicene or Apostles' Creed. At the end of the Liturgy of the Word, the congregation recites the Prayer of the Faithful, in which calls for special intercessions may be made.

∞ 84 ∞

LITURGY OF THE EUCHARIST

The second major part of the Mass reflects Christ's actions at the Last Supper and fulfills His request that His followers eat bread and drink wine as His body and blood in memory of His life, death, and Resurrection.

At this point, the priest will spend a few minutes going about the Preparation and Offering of the Gifts. There is an Offertory song, a kind of brief anthem, and Preparation of the Altar, the bread, and the wine. This includes folding special cloths to catch any fragments of bread or drops of wine once they are consecrated; mixing a little water with the wine; and getting the communion wafers, or "hosts," ready for the assembly.

The priest washes his hands, suggesting purification, and invites the assembly to prayer. As he turns back to the Gifts, the faithful say one brief prayer, and then what Catholics consider the awe-inspiring moment takes place. The Eucharistic Prayer, a prayer of thanksgiving, is spoken.

The Eucharistic Prayer consists of: an introductory Dialogue, Preface

(Lord Be With You), Sanctus, Thanksgiving, Acclamation, Epiclesis (the priest asks God to consecrate the host and wine), the Narrative Institution (the moment of consecration), the Anamnesis (that Christ comes to us through the Apostles), the Offering (Jesus offered to His Father), Petitions or Intercessions for the people, Doxology (or the Gloria in Excelsis: the angels' song at the birth of Our Lord), Memorial Acclamation, and Great Amen. This is the high point of the Mass, as the gifts of bread and wine become the Body and Blood of Christ in transubstantiation.

At that point, the Mass turns to the Communion Rite itself, which begins with the recitation of the Our Father, also known as the Lord's Prayer. Then, members of the assembly turn to each other to give the Rite of Peace, a sign that they are one with each other and that the Holy Spirit unites them. The Rite of Peace, originally The Kiss of Peace, descended from the Apostles, but at one time it was dropped from the liturgy. Vatican II reinstated it in the 1960s. Now called the Rite or even the Sign of Peace, it is not literally a kiss anymore, although family members and close friends attending Mass together often do exchange hugs and kisses at this point. Otherwise, parishioners usually shake hands with those next to them, saying "Peace be with you."

In the Fraction Rite, the priest "breaks" the bread (an actual loaf of bread is no longer used). The assembly says a prayer called the Agnus Dei (Lamb of God). The priest says a private prayer to prepare himself, and then he shows the host to the assembled and they humble themselves with a short prayer: "Lord, I am not worthy to receive you, but only say the word, and I shall be healed." At this point, everyone moves in procession to the sanctuary at the front of the church to receive communion. The Liturgy of the Eucharist ends with a prayer after Communion. Once the Mass is concluded, the priest blesses the congregation before they are dismissed.

∽ 85 ∽

LITURGY OF THE HOURS

The Liturgy of the Hours is a liturgy of prayers for every day of the year, with prayers assigned for particular times of each day. Priests, laypeople, and those belonging to Holy Orders are all encouraged to follow the Hours. All the prayers, hymns, psalms, and readings can be found in the Breviary, a voluminous compendium of prayers used by the clergy.

The tradition of the Hours goes all the way back to the early days of the Church, when monks and priests prayed every morning at sunrise and every evening at sundown. The Book of Psalms forms the basis of the Liturgy of Hours. Over the years, prayers, songs, psalms, and meditations were added to the original contents of the psalter.

At first, bishops and choirs chose the psalm that seemed suitable for the occasion, as different psalms might be better suited to morning or evening prayer, or to particular feast days. At one time, monks tried to recite all of the 150 psalms in one day. When this turned out to be too time-consuming, the recitation was spread out over a week, each day divided into hours.

In the 1960s, Vatican II revised and formalized the system of prayers, and the Liturgy of the Hours became known as "Divine Office." Now, once a year, Catholics can get a published work with the prayer structure formalized and laid out—with special psalms for particular feast and saints' days—so that all Catholics can worship in the same way.

In a single day, the Divine Office consists of Lauds and Vespers for morning; Matins, a prayer that may be recited at any point during the day; Terce, Sext, and None, prayers for midmorning, noon, and midafternoon; and Compline, which is the night prayer. In cathedrals and monasteries, Mass is celebrated after the Terce (which is said at the "third hour," or 9 A.M.)

∞ 86 ∞

IMPORTANT OBJECTS USED DURING MASS

The use of beautiful objects heightens the drama of any solemn ritual or occasion, and the Mass is no exception. First among sacred vessels, the **chalice** is the large cup that holds the wine that becomes the blood of Christ during the Eucharistic ceremony. The chalice must be made of either gold or silver. If it is silver, the bowl is gilded on the inside. A bishop must consecrate a chalice before it is used, and only priests and deacons are permitted to hold it.

The chalice has a long, rich history in the Church. Beautiful artifacts from the Middle Ages still exist, so the development of this wide-based, sumptuously decorated, sometimes double-handled vessel can easily be traced through the centuries to its present-day form.

The **paten** is a shallow, saucer-shaped disk used to hold bread that becomes the body of Christ. The paten, too, must be made of precious metal. In the earliest days of the Church, patens weighed as much as twenty-five pounds. Today they weigh only about a pound.

The chalice and paten have adjuncts (additional components) that perform certain functions.

Pall: A stiff, square piece of white linen that is placed over the chalice. The pall also requires a special blessing.

Purificator: A white linen cloth resembling a napkin, used to wipe and dry the chalice, or the priest's lips, after the ablutions.

Corporal: A white linen cloth, smaller than the breadth of the altar, on which the priest places the Sacred Host and the chalice during Mass.

Burse: A cover to keep the corporal from getting dirty; it has only been used since the sixteenth century.

Veil: The veil issued to cover the chalice and paten when they are brought to the altar.

The **ciborium** is a sacred cuplike vessel that holds the hosts once they have been consecrated. The ciborium is used to distribute Holy Communion to the faithful and is also used to keep the consecrated particles of the Blessed Sacrament in the tabernacle. Like the chalice and paten, it must be made of a precious metal and consecrated by a bishop. It differs from the chalice in that it is raised in the middle, so that the remaining blessed particles may be removed easily.

The **decanter**, or flagon, is a vessel brought forth with the gifts at the early part of the Mass. It holds the wine that will be consecrated for the communion of the people.

Communion cups are used infrequently, when the people receive wine at communion.

∞ 87 ∞

Marking time in the Catholic calendar

The liturgical calendar is a way of making time, which is an essential part of creation, sacred. This highly developed structure that encompasses the entire year did not exist in the early Church. Sunday, the day for celebration of the Eucharist, contained the essential elements of the entire year—the Passion, Death, and Resurrection—so the "paschal festival" was renewed every Sunday. On the annual anniversary, though, the day would be celebrated with great solemnity, and eventually Easter became the focal point of the liturgical year. The feast of Easter was clearly linked to that of the Pentecost, the festival celebrating the Descent of the Holy Spirit on the disciples fifty days after Easter.

Today, some feast days are fixed while others are based on seasonal changes and moon phases, which means that the liturgical calendar fluctuates from year to year. For instance, the date for Easter is linked to the spring equinox. Every year, the date changes—Easter Sunday always occurs on the Sunday after the full moon following the equinox. Christmas, however, is fixed on December 25.

Furthermore, the Church year consists of two distinct cycles, the temporal cycle and the sanctoral cycle. The temporal cycle is a series of solemn events celebrating the mystery of Christ—Advent, Christmas, Lent, Holy Week, Easter—divided into two cycles (the Christmas cycle and the Easter cycle), plus what the Church calls ordinary time, or the remainder of the year. The sanctoral cycle includes all the saints' feast days and many of the Marian feast days.

Each liturgical season has its own symbolic color: violet for Advent, white for the Christmas season, green for Epiphany, violet (again) for Lent, white and gold for Easter, and red for Pentecost. These colors appear in the vestments of the clergy and in church decorations.

The liturgical calendar includes Sunday celebrations and holy days of obligation, which commemorate special events or persons of high reverence. The days of chief importance in this group are called solemnities. Some of these solemnities may be part of a larger cycle, such as the Epiphany.

The solemnities for the full liturgical year include the following:

January 1: Mary, Mother of God
January 6: Epiphany
March 25: Annunciation
May or June (Sunday after Pentecost): Holy Trinity

Sunday after Holy Trinity Sunday: Corpus Christi
Thursday forty days after Easter (or the Sunday after it): Ascension
Friday following second Sunday after Pentecost: Sacred Heart
June 24: Birth of John the Baptist
June 30: First Martyrs of the Church of Rome
August 15: Assumption
November 1: All Saints
Last Sunday in ordinary time: Christ the King
December 8: Immaculate Conception

Feast days are saints' days or days celebrating the Virgin Mary; generally, they are days of lesser significance that sprang from the people, not the Church. (It should be noted that some of the Marian devotions have been elevated in importance.) Memorials are less significant, and not obligatory. For instance, Mark the Evangelist's feast day is April 25, while Catherine of Siena is honored with a memorial day on April 29.

∽∽ 88 ∽∽

ADVENT AND CHRISTMAS:
ANTICIPATING AND CELEBRATING CHRIST'S ARRIVAL

The Church year begins with the Christmas cycle, which encompasses the events surrounding Jesus' birth. The Christmas cycle starts with

Advent, which begins on the Sunday closest to November 30, the feast day of St. Andrew the Apostle; and ends with the baptism of the Lord (third Sunday after Christmas), which celebrates the beginning of Christ's public ministry.

Advent literally means "arrival," and in the Church, Advent is a four-week season of preparation that anticipates the upcoming birth of Christ. It is a season of mixed themes—both penance and joy. The Advent wreath, with its four candles, symbolizes the end of darkness and the turning toward light in the coming of the Lord.

The word *Christmas* is derived from the phrase "Mass of Christ" because the Church holds special Masses on Christmas Eve and Christmas morning. Catholics celebrate Christmas, or the Nativity of Jesus, on December 25. However, Jesus' actual birthday is not known. One of the explanations for why the Church chose this particular day is that in early times, some of the Church's feast days were appropriated from previous pagan celebrations. In the case of Christmas, this particular date was also chosen because it is the time of the winter solstice. This point, after which the days grow longer little by little and light once again begins to prevail over darkness, fits well symbolically with the light of Christ coming into the world.

Following Christmas, the Epiphany, celebrated on January 6, commemorates the arrival of the three wise men who came bearing gifts to honor the newborn Christ Child in the manger. *Epiphany* literally means "to show," "to make known," or "to reveal," and as a part of the Christmas season, it represents the revealing of Jesus as Lord and King.

The Christmas cycle ends on the third Sunday after Christmas. A period of ordinary time ensues that lasts until the day after Mardi Gras, the beginning of the Easter cycle.

∽∾ 89 ∽∾

LENT AND EASTER: BUILDING TOWARD THE MOST IMPORTANT CATHOLIC FEAST

The Easter cycle comprises two periods: Lent and Easter. Lent begins on Ash Wednesday, the day after a popular Catholic festival known as the Mardi Gras (French for "Fat Tuesday"), a day of carnivals and celebrations. In contrast, Ash Wednesday is a somber day. One popular custom is for parishioners to mark their foreheads with a thumbprint of ash from burned palms, reminding them of their sins. After Ash Wednesday, Lent continues for a forty-day period of fasting, abstinence, and prayer. The last day of Lent is the Thursday before Easter.

The Catholic Church used to shroud statues and other icons as a way of showing mourning during the whole somber season of Lent and to hide the glory of the triumphant Christ. Today, this practice is generally limited to the fifth Sunday of Lent.

The greatest of all Catholic feasts takes place during Holy Week, the center of the Church year. Holy Week begins with Palm Sunday, the day of Jesus' arrival in Jerusalem, when He rode in on a donkey and was welcomed by people waving palm branches. Despite the joy of this reception, the purpose is to remember the suffering Jesus was about to endure.

In the following week, Holy Thursday celebrates the Last Supper, at which Jesus first instructed the disciples to celebrate the Eucharist by breaking bread and drinking wine in memory of Him. The following day, Good Friday, marks the anniversary of Jesus' crucifixion. On Holy Saturday, churches hold a special Mass, and during the night Catholics hold the Easter Vigil, which anticipates Jesus' Resurrection on the following day—the glorious day of Easter Sunday. Fifty days after Easter Sunday, the Church celebrates Pentecost, which is when the Holy Spirit descended to the disciples. Apostle Pentecost completes the Easter cycle, and another period of ordinary time follows until the next Advent.

∽∽ 90 ∽∽

CONVERTING TO CATHOLICISM

People who convert are seekers. Intellectually, spiritually, or emotionally, they are looking for a faith that satisfies a deep need within them. The Rite of Christian Initiation for Adults (RCIA), a process by which adults can convert to Catholicism, is important, and the Church has prepared guidelines for how it should be carried out.

The Church has an obligation to receive any convert who professes the Catholic faith, regardless of previous religion, age, sex, or background, but it lays down some conditions. Those who are interested in converting must learn about the religion, profess the faith, and make a commitment to live in accordance with Catholic teaching.

The first step to becoming a Catholic is contacting the nearest Catholic parish. A pastor or religious educator will meet with those interested in converting and advise them of the required steps. Parishes usually offer the RCIA, and in most parishes, the process begins in September and ends during Holy Week.

Most adults begin their conversion with a period of intense study to gain a sufficient understanding of Catholicism. Seekers are expected to ask hard questions about Christianity and Catholic dogma. Adults may be paired with mentors, usually other adults living in the faith who can help answer their questions. The informal discussions during the inquiry period help seekers determine whether they can live with the rules and teachings of the Catholic community.

In addition, after they have received the permission of a local bishop, new converts participate in three important rites: the Rite of Acceptance, Rite of Election, and Sacraments of Initiation.

The Rite of Acceptance is held several times each year at Sunday Mass. At this ceremony, inquirers are marked with the sign of the cross on the ears, eyes, lips, heart, shoulders, hands, and feet—a symbol of both the joys and the costs of Christian discipleship. This ritual begins their period of catechumenate.

Catechumenates join Sunday Mass during the Liturgy of the Word, after which they move to another place to continue reflecting on the

Scriptures. This period of study varies according to individual need. Catholic children are expected to have at least two years of study in preparation for their Confirmation. The norm for adults is a year or more.

The catechumenate period ends with the Rite of Election. This rite is held on the first Sunday in Lent. In a ceremony performed by the bishop of the diocese, catechumens receive the Call to Continuing Conversion.

Before the Sacraments of Initiation can be administered, however, the catechumens (now known as the Elect) must undergo a final period of purification and enlightenment. The Elect spend the period during the forty days of Lent in intense prayer and preparation. They are expected to repent of past sins and to reflect on their character and on their readiness to join the Church.

The Elect participate in several other rituals, called scrutinies, on Sundays throughout Lent. The scrutinies are rites for self-searching and repentance, whose aim is to heal qualities that are weak or sinful while strengthening those that are positive and strong. During this period, the Elect are also formally presented with the Apostles' Creed and the Lord's Prayer, both of which they recite on the night they are initiated.

The Sacraments of Initiation—Baptism, Confirmation, and Eucharist—integrate the formal process by which adults are finally admitted to the Catholic Church. These are usually performed at the Easter Vigil on Holy Saturday. Only people who have never been baptized in a Christian church undergo all three sacraments.

In the fifty days following the celebration of Christian initiation, newly baptized converts continue their program of Christian formation.

They can participate fully with the faithful in Eucharist and in the mission of the Church for justice and peace. This period of *mystagogy* normally lasts until Pentecost Sunday.

People who have already been baptized at another Christian church must undertake a different kind of preparation for the Sacraments of Initiation. The Church may insist on separation of these people from the catechumens. The needs of mature, practicing Christians from other faith traditions are considered on an individual basis. Those who have lived as Christians and who only need instruction in the Catholic tradition are called candidates and do not undergo the full program.

Their journey includes receiving the sacrament of Penance (confession) before receiving Confirmation, undergoing a period of training and inquiry, and joining services for the Liturgy of the Word. On the first Sunday in Lent, the candidates participate in the Celebration of the Call to Continuing Conversion.

During this purification and enlightenment process, candidates are expected to participate in a penitential rite as well as a period of reflection. Because candidates who previously were baptized in a Christian church will have committed sins since their baptism, they must confess their mortal sins before receiving Confirmation. Reception into full communion in the Catholic Church takes place with the profession of faith, Confirmation, and Eucharist during a Sunday Mass with their local parish.

FAMOUS CONVERSIONS FROM PAST AND MODERN TIMES

One of Christianity's most enduring images is St. Paul's conversion on the road to Damascus. A zealous Jew, Paul (then known as Saul) had just witnessed the stoning of Stephen. While traveling to Damascus, he was struck down by a bright light. He heard the voice of Jesus telling him to stop the persecution of Christians and to take up ministry. The event left Saul blind for three days, until one of Jesus' followers laid hands on him and he was able to see again. With his new sight, Saul gained a new faith. He dropped his Jewish name in favor of the Romanized Paul and began preaching Christianity. Paul was one of the most prolific writers of the early Church.

Another saint, one of Christianity's great philosophers, St. Augustine, born in what is now Algeria in 354, also converted back to Catholicism after abandoning his faith in favor of philosophy and an easy, immoral lifestyle. Augustine was a young professor of rhetoric in Milan when he discovered the philosophy of Plotinus and St. Paul. He eventually returned to North Africa, where he adopted a monastic lifestyle. He was later ordained a bishop. St. Augustine's meditations on the nature of grace and his books, *Confessions* and *City of God,* remain influential today.

Many royal conversions also took place, such as those of the fourth-century Roman emperor Constantine, who prohibited persecution of Christians, and Theodosius, who declared that all of Rome should be Christian and granted privileges to the Catholic clergy.

King Henry IV of France (1553–1610), who was raised a Huguenot and participated in the War of Religions that split France, became heir to the throne in 1584. When the powerful Catholic League refused to accept a Protestant on the throne, Henry then converted to Catholicism, in one of history's more controversial conversions. King Charles II of England (1630–1685) converted on his deathbed after a reign marked by efforts to win religious tolerance.

In the middle of the nineteenth century, many British thinkers and theologians converted to Catholicism under the influence of the Oxford, or Tractarian, movement, formed among scholars at Oxford University who decried the liberalism of the Anglican church and worried about political trends that threatened its influence on English society. One of the leaders of the Oxford movement, John Henry Newman, converted to Catholicism in 1845 at age forty-four and went on to become a cardinal in the Church.

Influenced by the Oxford movement while studying there, the poet Gerard Manley Hopkins converted in 1866 and joined the Jesuit Order. Hopkins worked among the poor and later became a preacher. He is best known for the original use of language in his religious poetry.

In America, Dorothy Day (1897–1980), moved by the poverty of working people, became active in left-wing and labor movements. In 1927, after the birth of a daughter, she converted to Catholicism but was disappointed by the Church's lack of support for workers. She founded the *Catholic Worker,* an inexpensive paper covering labor news, during the Great Depression, while simultaneously operating a soup kitchen to help the thousands of unemployed.

The *Catholic Worker* took a pacifist stance during World War II, and it opposed the excesses of the Cold War. Unsurprisingly, Day was an early opponent of the Vietnam War and a supporter of Cesar Chavez's farm workers' movement. Her paper had a wide following among young activists and support from Church peace movements.

Thomas Merton, one of the most influential American spiritual writers of the twentieth century, described the process of his conversion in *The Seven Storey Mountain*. A Trappist monk (one of the most ascetic orders), he was influential in the peace movement of the 1960s and interested in Eastern religions, promoting dialogue between the East and the West.

One of the best-known recent converts is Malcolm Muggeridge. A former editor of *Punch,* he was also a journalist and commentator. Furthermore, Muggeridge is credited with making Mother Teresa's work known to the world in his role as the British Broadcasting Corporation producer of the 1968 documentary, *Something Beautiful for God*.

Many other famous individuals have converted to Catholicism, including novelists, poets, essayists, and social historians. Among them are G. K. Chesterton (1874–1936); Alice Meynell (1847–1922); Alfred Noyes (1880–1958); Robert Lowell (1917–1977); Graham Greene (1904–1991); and Evelyn Waugh (1903–1966).

Today, prominent individuals continue to seek out the Catholic Church. Among American converts, such as Scott Hahn, David Currie, and Patrick Madrid, there is a tradition of confessional literature, in which writers tell of their own struggles with faith and their reasons for turning to Catholicism.

Part 6

CONTEMPORARY
ISSUES CONFRONTING
CATHOLICS

THE MESSAGE OF JESUS AND OF THE GOSPELS THAT TELL HIS story will always remain the same. However, the interpretation of Christ's message changes along with developments in human understanding. The Church is not stagnant in its thinking—it is constantly transforming, as it grows in its understanding of Christ's love.

As previously explained, the Catholic religion is not a faith based on belief alone. Catholicism is an active, dynamic faith that calls each member to be aware of issues that affect the world and to work for change where necessary. First and foremost, all Catholic individuals receive a call to ministry by virtue of their being Catholic. Through Baptism and Confirmation, Catholics are joined in Christ with the Church and work the ministry of Christ in their own special ways. Outside of organized lay work, Catholics have ample opportunity to offer services in their own parishes. They can help a sick neighbor, organize a bake sale for their church or parish school, teach a children's class at Sunday School, drive food baskets around at Christmas, assist the church with donations, or simply carry the offering plate during Mass. There are dozens of small ways to help out. These Catholic heroes may go unsung, but they are the pillars of the church, what Vatican II called "the salt of the earth."

Today, the Church continues to stay abreast of contemporary issues and create inroads to act as a voice of sound morality and justice for the world; to create greater opportunity for members' participation; to improve communication with all faiths; and to improve the quality of life for all human beings throughout the entire world.

∞ 92 ∞

CONTEMPORARY CHALLENGES AND OPENNESS TO CHANGE

Since Vatican II, the winds of change have blown through the Catholic Church. Although they have blown away some of the cobwebs, they have also caused major upheaval in certain areas.

Despite an emphasis on the collegiality of bishops, and on greater participation of the faithful, the Catholic Church still has an authoritarian, hierarchical structure that sometimes incites feelings of anger and alienation among the faithful in every rank. Although there are more Catholics now than ever, and their numbers continue to grow, there is a decline in vocations to both the priesthood and to religious orders.

Celibacy is no doubt an issue, but the clergy has also lost its revered status and its special place in the hierarchy. With the acceptance of the idea of the universal priesthood of Christ, the clergy is now merely a subset of the priesthood of the faithful. With fewer young seminarians and priests coming in, an ever-growing number of ailing and elderly priests must be cared for. This is a drain on the financial and personal resources of the Church. With fewer priests to look after parishes, there also are fewer priests to staff the missionary endeavors of the Church.

The Church has developed a number of strategies to help remedy some of the current problems facing the ministry. It has adopted techniques for determining who is qualified to handle the demanding role of diocesan priests and has improved the education programs in seminaries that prepare men for the priesthood. The Church also has encouraged bishops to provide support for their priests.

The Church is also confronting the Catholic dissatisfaction with its rigid stands on birth control and divorce. The Church does not permit any form of artificial contraception, but many clergymen at high levels within the Church do recommend it. Divorced Catholics are not allowed to remarry while their partners are still alive, and if they do, they are not allowed to receive the sacraments. Regardless, some pastors have gone so far as to bless second marriages, even though they could not marry the couple.

Individually, the clergy recognize the gray areas that exist in marriage and family life. Prominent theologians have concurred that singular moral rules and moral judgments cannot be applied to humanity as a whole. Where there is a human relationship, each case must be judged on its own merits.

Despite the Church's authoritarian structure and tradition, there now is more debate and dissension as well as openness to new ways of thinking and approaching issues dealing with morality, tradition, ecumenism, and interreligious dialogue. Theologians are coming to acknowledge that doctrines reflect the tenor of the times in and must be interpreted as such, and Catholic dialogue with other faiths has made great strides.

Despite its problems, the Church remains vigorous and healthy, and it continues to display the four qualities by which it has come to be defined. It is catholic in its embrace of all humanity; it is one in its common beliefs; it is holy in its union with the Father, Son, and Holy Spirit; and it is apostolic in its succession, tradition, and ongoing mission.

∾ 93 ∾

THE CALL TO RELIGIOUS LIFE

The Catholic Church teaches that we share in the tasks of Christ, and, as such, we share in the "common priesthood of the faithful" (as the Catechism of the Catholic Church terms it). This means a general call to the laity to share and spread the Word of God. But beyond this general call, there is the special call to the ordained priesthood: the sacrament of Holy Orders (see Number 59).

Priests preach Christ's Gospel in their efforts to bring people to Catholic maturity. Once they are ordained, priests are, in a sense, set apart. This helps them dedicate themselves to God's ministry with complete devotion. Laypeople who take on the important work of assisting priests help them in being the leaders of the faithful that they need to be.

Until about twenty-five years ago, it was very common among ardent Catholic families for at least one son to choose the priesthood. It was a badge of honor, and for boys raised in an atmospheric Catholic environment, the call to the priesthood was often glamorous and appealing.

Nowadays, the secular world has greatly encroached on the call to Holy Orders. Catholics live in a culture that trivializes religion and instead exalts consumerism, materialism, and moral relativism. There are more distractions, and hence fewer men are joining the priesthood. It is difficult in such a busy world to heed a call or indeed even to be aware of it.

Men who do respond to the religious calling go through a variety of stages before they are anointed. They do a lot of thinking—and praying. After these men are accepted into the seminary, they undergo many tests of doubt before they are sure their vocation is true.

It isn't easy being a priest in today's world. There are many complex problems to deal with. Priests have to counsel women about birth control and abortion. Families seem to be under particular stress. Sometimes the priest must take on the role of a social worker, conducting marital therapy sessions or helping children of broken homes.

It takes a man with a particular set of skills to deal with both the ministry and the mission, especially in dynamic urban centers. Today's

Catholics have easy access to almost every temptation there is. Even some priests themselves are, at times, drawn into behaviors that are utterly unacceptable and scandalous—the recent pedophile scandal being a prime example. Conscientious, concerned priests must be prepared to counsel their parishioners regarding a broad spectrum of problems; they need to be sophisticated enough to understand this world and to help guide their assemblies through it.

Knowing whether you have a calling is called "discernment." Certain questions and considerations, such as whether a person is meant for a religious calling or the vocation of marriage, come up time and again for those considering the priesthood. Those who go into religious orders have to take vows of chastity, poverty, and obedience. Understandably, this can be difficult—and upsetting to family and friends. These types of questions also apply to women who consider becoming nuns. It is an agonizing choice for young people, and one not easily made.

Once he achieves a certain degree of certainty, a young man must then seek guidance from a priest he trusts. The priest's guidance will help him figure out whether he has really experienced the call to priesthood. The next step is to enroll in a seminary or to join a religious order that most closely corresponds to the young man's religious aims or convictions.

Catholics also have the option to join a religious order and do ministry work as monks or nuns in hospitals, missions, parishes, prisons, schools, seminaries, and universities, to name a few.

Becoming a member of a religious order is a demanding vocation. Life is completely ordered within the hierarchy of the organization, and each person must be able to fit into that hierarchy and submit to its authority. "Vowed" orders take vows of chastity, obedience, and poverty.

Those who choose to join a religious order must find an organization that appeals to what they would like to do, whether it's work in a faraway mission or a monastic life of seclusion. Those considering joining an order should examine their doubts and weigh their choices carefully.

∽∽ 94 ∽∽

Reforming Church structure

The current office of the Bishop of Rome still retains the trappings of a feudal monarchy. No matter how hard the pope and the cardinals try to engage with the world, they are limited by a strict notion of hierarchy. The most responsive faith experiences are initiated first among the priests and the laity. They reach the ears of the bishops only later and only when the Spirit opens their hearts to change.

Vatican II set trends in motion that have already changed the role of the papacy, however, beginning with a redefinition of infallibility. Infallibility is expressed by the belief of the people of the Church, all of whom are in union with the popes and bishops. The people have to believe and accept a teaching for it to be a true belief. In his role as the visible head of the Church, the pope is infallible in teaching Christ's message and in his moral rulings, but it has been acknowledged that he can err.

The idea that the pope can sin and make mistakes in governing the Church or ruling on temporal matters opens the door to a different kind of papacy. Even moral and religious teachings of the past can be reformed, if they are not taught by a consensus of theologians and received by the people of the Church. This may lighten the heavy load of tradition within the Church and allow later popes to lead the Church in a new direction.

The change would have to rest on a reformed Church structure in which the voices of the laity reach the top more quickly. The laity is already playing a stronger role in the Church because of the shortage of new priests. If laypeople succeed in creating structures at the national Church level that are more responsive to lay concerns, they could begin to dissolve the hierarchy. The pope would remain a spiritual leader, reinterpreting Christ's message for every age with the help of the Holy Spirit, but Church structures would be decided and operated by laypeople.

The papacy might be a movable office under this new regime. Perhaps national Church leaders would elect popes for a fixed term of five or ten years. The seat of the Holy See itself could shift around the world with the nationality of the current pope, becoming a movable Vatican. Within this view, the role of the pope would be that of a peacemaker, mediator, and ethical counselor who fosters dialogue and keeps communication lines open among different parts of the world.

Other Christian churches have models for more democratic leadership, but none has a spiritual leader of the stature of the pope. One of the Church's goals is unity among Christians. As of now, no one has yet suggested a course that would bring all Christians together.

In a less reform-oriented Church, there is a different danger for the papacy—the widening rift between the liberal Western democratic ideals of Europe and the increasingly dominant representatives of developing countries. This could split the Catholic world, with the Western Church rejecting the authority of Rome, if not in words, at least in action. The papacy would then lose its spiritual hold over the hemisphere that dominates world economies and become less influential in its teachings.

∾ 95 ∾

PRESSURE FOR DEMOCRATIZATION AND INCREASED DIVERSITY

The current pontiff, Pope John Paul II, has a reputation as a conservative leader who approves of the hierarchical structure of the Catholic institution and prefers a small group of cardinals to set agendas, which are then passed down to the bishops and parishes.

However, Vatican II did rule that the laity has a role in accepting the teachings of the Church. This is because, in essence, the Church *is* the whole people of God. Pope John Paul II has made little progress in implementing this new direction for the Church, leading to tension between the Church hierarchy and the laity. There is pressure for democratization, particularly from people living in democracies. Most are simply asking for a way of expressing their concerns and jointly developing solutions that work in the real world they live in.

In the United States in particular, there has been a disconnection between the institutional Church and its people. In the past thirty-five years, the idea of obedience to the Church has fallen into disregard. People walk their own paths over sexual mores, prohibitions on using birth control, and the Church's approach to poverty and health care. While it's not hard to find people who call themselves Catholic, it is harder to find those who obey the Church in every aspect. Many people today accept the faith, but they are not comfortable with the structure of the Church.

Today, dissent is still strongly discouraged, and those who openly discuss controversial issues like the ordination of women are disciplined. Theologians in independent universities need a contract from the bishops to continue with their teaching, and these contracts may be revoked if the scholars investigate new ways of thinking. Married couples who view sex as a way of reaffirming their love, rather than a mere necessity for procreation, are told they are sinful. These are problems of a Church whose teaching is dictated from the top, with little reference to the parish priest or lay believer.

However, it seems that the gradual democratization of the Church is a strong possibility, given the commitment of many lay Catholics and their growing presence in the workings of the Church. Many Catholics hope that the Holy Spirit will help guide the Church toward a more inclusive attitude toward its laity and a review of the Church hierarchy.

The Church is also no longer predominantly Western, European, and white. As it moves away from its European traditions, it is pressed to be more multicultural and diverse in its practices and liturgies. Church concerns may also change to reflect the strength of the Latin American and

African clergy and the issues they are dealing with, including poverty, AIDS, human rights, and the exploitation of resources.

The reality of greater cultural diversity, particularly in Africa, where more than sixty languages are spoken, is likely to push the Church in new directions. As it grows, it seeks ways to honor traditional African customs and ways of thinking within the Church community. Already more of the priesthood is indigenous, as a result of a push in the 1980s to educate and recruit young people. The most challenging aspect of the Church's mission in Africa is how to serve society in the face of human rights violations, war, famine, and disease.

In the Western world, great affluence and a decline in religious thinking has created an atmosphere in which people feel spiritually lost. New models of worship are pulling in groups such as divorced Catholics, who thought they no longer had a place within the Church. European and American churches are experimenting with small faith groups, prayer circles, and innovative liturgies and services.

∞ 96 ∞

THE LOCAL PARISH: THE HEART OF CATHOLIC LIFE

In the United States, immigrants from the Old World who settled in neighborhoods with their former countrymen formed many Catholic communities. They raised their children in tight neighborhoods that reflected their values. At the center of these communities was the parish, a reliable support mechanism that, in turn, centered on a priest and a church. Often, the parish formed its own social institutions.

The Church begins its work in the world at the parish level through programs for youth, charitable work, and pastoral care. Catholics value community in part because it is one of the tools God uses to work for good in the world. Various overlapping networks that link people together have evolved out of parish life. including not only religious organizations but also social, civil, fraternal, and political groups.

Catholics also turn to their parish for support in their spiritual life and to establish strong personal relationships that carry them through times of trouble. They want their children to be part of a community that shares the same values. The parish is a vehicle for getting involved in charitable work, but it is also increasingly a place to get involved in organizations that back a moral cause, such as pro-life, social-justice, or environmental groups. Inner-city parishes are still dealing with problems of poverty and congregations of recent immigrants, but many Catholics now live in the suburbs, and their parishes are challenged to deal with the problems that accompany affluence.

The parish is where people live, die, marry, baptize their babies, educate their children, and make lifelong friends. The latest news from the Vatican or the position papers of the bishops are of less significance. Even the birth-control encyclical, which significantly reduced church attendance and donations, can be dismissed by Catholics who disagree with it if they feel at home in their parish.

The parish priest is the heart of a successful parish. But the laypeople who keep things going in a parish usually outlast their priests. As the number of priests in the United States declines, the role of the laity in parish life increases in importance. Laypeople help distribute communion and prepare for worship, get involved with local schools, visit members of the congregation who are ill, and operate Catholic charities. As the role of women in the society has changed, Catholic women have also insisted on playing leadership roles in worship, charitable organizations, and school councils.

Within middle-class communities, there is pressure to experiment with more modern styles of worship. Some are pressing their priest for sermons more rooted in the world. Some parishes are heavily involved in political issues such as homelessness, poverty, and minority rights. Active parishes are pushing against the strictures of a conservative Church that has not abandoned its traditional hierarchical structure.

∽∾ 97 ∽∾

SUPPORT OF CATHOLIC EDUCATION AND THE GROWTH OF CATHOLIC COLLEGES AND UNIVERSITIES

Catholic families continue to send their children to Catholic elementary and high schools in record numbers, and some schools in suburban areas actually have waiting lists. Catholic education appears to make a significant difference in religious and moral behavior, with Catholic-educated young adults more likely to continue attending church and to be more sexually conservative.

The first Catholic schools in North America were founded by religious orders to train the young in reading and religion and to select candidates for the seminary. Parishes took over the task of establishing schools in the 1800s as Catholic immigrants streamed into American cities. In the United States, Catholic parochial schools remained under the control of the Church, and they have never attained full access to public funding.

The Church views Catholic education as an important tool for setting a moral foundation for the young. Religious education and lessons on applying Catholic faith and morality in daily life are important parts of the curriculum. At the same time, there is an emphasis on academic excellence; many students continue their education at colleges and universities.

The earliest Catholic universities in Europe operated under papal charter, among them the University of Paris, Oxford University, and the University of Bologna. In the eleventh and twelfth centuries, groups of scholars or clergy in the large cities gathered together to exchange ideas. In the thirteenth century, these centers of learning sought papal charters or royal charters, so both civil and religious authorities played a role in the founding of the great universities. These places of learning taught the law, the arts and philosophy, medicine, and theology.

In the New World, the earliest Catholic colleges were established as a way of training priests and nuns in their vocations. But after 1900, higher education started gaining momentum as Catholics began to recognize the power that education had to encourage upward mobility. Catholic colleges and universities were created to compete with secular and Protestant institutions and to continue the work of the parochial schools in forming young men and women as "citizens for the city of God." The colleges were under the control of religious orders and staffed by priests or nuns. The teaching approach was conservative, emphasizing Catholic doctrine and limiting opportunities for women to teaching, nursing, social work, and home economy.

Following World War II, many young men flowed into the universities on the G.I. Bill. These former soldiers were interested in improving their career prospects. Pressured to provide superior education, Catholic colleges and universities sought to improve the quality of Catholic education and brought in laypeople to teach secular subjects like science and technology.

During the 1960s, universities and colleges sought separate incorporation. The Church's tight control was broken, and independent boards began building institutions such as the University of Notre Dame, Fordham University, and Georgetown University into some of the best schools in the United States. In the 1970s, the universities gained access to federal funding on the same basis as other institutions of higher learning.

A more secular environment left campuses struggling with secular issues—such as whom to hire and whether Catholic faith should be a prerequisite; how to improve the opportunities for minority groups; and how to handle academic freedom. Many lay professors who joined these institutions assumed the right to academic freedom. Yet professors who spoke freely, especially on issues such as contraception and abortion, found themselves on a collision course with the Vatican.

The Vatican moved to reassert some kind of control, demanding that professors who teach theological studies be appointed with approval of the local bishops. Pope John Paul II's 1990 document on the relationship between universities and the Church, *Ex Corde Ecclesiae,* renewed this demand but left this tension between the academic community and the Vatican unresolved.

Many of the students who streamed into Catholic universities throughout the 1970s are now affluent alumni who can support their alma maters. The United States now has 238 Catholic colleges and universities providing higher education to more than 600,000 students. They are located in forty of the fifty states and include—among many—the University of Saint Louis and the University of New Rochelle.

Many of the nineteen Catholic colleges of Canada have merged with the public university system, including St. Michael's College, now part of the University of Toronto; St. Jerome's at University of Waterloo; and St. Paul's at the University of Manitoba.

∽ 98 ∽

Laity involvement and the issue of female ordination

Laymen and -women are taking increasingly sophisticated jobs within the Church, including those that used to be performed by priests and members of religious orders. Since older members of religious orders are retiring, and fewer men and women are seeking life as monks or nuns, laypeople are stepping up to fill the void.

In the liturgy, laypeople take on the role of cantors, music directors, readers, altar servers, and Eucharistic ministers. Some even lead Sunday worship in the absence of a priest. They teach youth and adults and participate in marriage preparations, ministry with divorced or separated Catholics, and bereavement programs. Some are involved in Catholic charities, peace and justice networks, soup kitchens, and shelters. They work in Catholic health-care and social-service institutions. Often these laypeople are responding to a call they feel to serve Christ and the Church and to live the Christian message. Although some Catholics have objected to receiving the Eucharist from a layperson or getting a pastoral visit from someone other than the priest, most accept these practices.

Despite these strides, laypeople are not allowed to consecrate the host or administer sacraments. These tasks continue to be reserved for ordained ministers only. In some cases, lay involvement in a parish's decision-making process is also restricted by the parish priest, local bishop, or even the Church officials at the national level.

In Europe and the Americas, where Catholic women have seen other Christian churches accept female ministry, the fact that women cannot be ordained as priests is one of the most significant points of contention. Catholics in these parts of the world are alarmed at the dearth of young men willing to train for the priesthood. Many women are willing to take on the ministry, and some have become better trained than priests.

Women played important roles in the Church throughout its early history as martyrs for the Christian faith, saints, and members of religious orders. However, they appear to have lost their leadership positions in the Church around the sixth century A.D.

Women began to ask for a more prominent role in the Church in the 1960s. In 1976, the Pontifical Biblical Commission reported that it could find no support in the biblical evidence for the exclusion of women from the ordained priesthood. However, both the pope and the American bishops have written letters saying that the ordination of women is not justified, and the issue continues to be debated.

The Church has, however, shifted its perception of women and their roles. Women are seen as equal in human dignity with men and are no longer subservient to men, nor are they expected to obey male authority. In 1995, Pope John Paul II said there was an urgent need to achieve equality in every area, and he further wrote that the process of women's liberation has been substantially positive.

As lay ministers, women are taking on tasks that were once limited to men, including everything from serving as lectors and Eucharistic ministers to running Catholic schools and charitable organizations. Feminist theology is now part of the curriculum in Catholic academia, and women may even teach in seminaries. Female theologians re-examine the Scriptures with fresh insights, reflecting on how Jesus Himself treated women with great respect and compassion and rejected the narrow, subservient role of women that was the norm in His day.

However, since the hierarchy draws its authority from being the spiritual descendants of the Apostles, the Church maintains that like the

Apostles, the clergy should be male. The counterargument is that Christ did not ordain anyone to be a priest, man or woman. Furthermore, He had many women among His followers; after His Resurrection, He appeared first to Mary Magdalene.

Many Catholics say that priests suffer in their understanding of the world by being cut off from close relationships with women. Priests cannot marry, are trained separately from women, and work mainly with other priests. While many parish priests develop an understanding of the problems of women's lives by ministering to women within their congregation, those who rise highest in the Church are much more isolated, a condition that some say leads to condescending and antifeminist attitudes.

The exclusively male hierarchy of the Church leads to decisions being made without any discussion from a female point of view, and this tends to work against the ordination of women. The Vatican II charge that the Church should become the whole people of God is contributing to a push for new understanding. If people are the Church, they might be able to effect a change, as long as they continue to seek ministry among women. If Christ calls everyone to use his or her skills to serve the Church, then women must follow this call as faithfully as men.

The call to responsible stewardship

The Church teaches that God created an ordered universe, and since it came out of His goodness, it was good. Therefore, human beings are bound to respect and defend the goodness of creation, including the physical world in which they live. God entrusted human beings with having dominion over the Earth. In return human beings must complete the work of creation and perfect it for the good of all.

Catholics believe that God expects humankind to exercise stewardship over the Earth. As God's highest creation, human beings have a responsibility to use their knowledge to preserve and protect the environment and the creatures who live in it. Both the Holy See and the U.S. Conference of Catholic Bishops have pressed for action in response to global warming and have urged governments to move toward models of sustainable development. In North America, the Church operates an "environmental justice" grants program that provides money for environmental education, research, and action. The Church's environmentalist stance is tied to its support for developing nations, as their growth hinges on an equitable sharing of the Earth's resources.

There is also fledgling lay movement for individual action to preserve the environment. This movement urges Catholics to live with respect for the rest of creation by practicing organic gardening, reducing automobile use, and consciously reducing consumption of material goods.

Catholic Catechism emphasizes the interdependence of all things as part of God's plan. Each plant and animal has its own particular goodness and perfection and should be respected as a work of creation. Making use of creation for our own livelihood is part of humankind's role, but each tree, plant, and animal must be taken with good reason and in a way that would not lead to disorder in the environment.

∽ 100 ∽

PROMOTING HUMAN RIGHTS AND CHARITABLE VALUES

The Catholic Church teaches that "the dignity of the human person is rooted in his creation in the image and likeness of God" (from the Catechism of the Catholic Church, 1997). Charity is a virtue that disposes people to love God above all else and to include their neighbors as part of that love. It knits people into the community and is meritorious of eternal life. According to Jesus' pronouncement, each good deed done for the benefit of another person is also done for Christ. That is because the person in need is a child of God.

The Church calls this service toward others "vocation to beatitude," and it is a duty of each Catholic person. (Vocation is a "call," and Catholics are called to help others.) The Catechism explains that the Beatitudes portray Christ's charity (see Number 7). Beautiful and paradoxical, the Beatitudes are precepts meant to comfort believers and inspire them to practice charity for the meek, the poor, the hungry, and disenfranchised, for whom Christ spoke so eloquently in His Sermon on the Mount.

The obligation to give to others is rooted in the message of the Gospels. Jesus tells us to treat our neighbors as we ourselves would like to be treated. The Church holds this message in mind as it lobbies in political forums, publishes encyclicals, and sends its charities out to work in the world. It seeks the unity of humankind through both a union of the spirit and the cultivation of equality for all people.

Jesus' own detachment from wealth and material possessions and His love of the poor are powerful themes of Christian life. Pope John Paul II often criticizes American culture, saying it puts financial profits ahead of all other values. Yet the drive to succeed financially and to build a better life for one's family is a staple of North American life. This poses an ethical dilemma for Catholics in business. In many situations, a business can operate in a way that is legally right yet morally questionable. However, business organizations such as Legatus (an international organization for Catholic businesspeople begun in Detroit); Business Leaders for Excellence, Ethics, and Judgment, in Chicago; and Civitas Dei in Indianapolis are bringing more talk about living the faith in the workplace.

Liberation theology, developed in the 1970s by a group of Latin American clerics, sees the Word of God mediated through the poor and oppressed. Only by participating in the struggles of these people can Christians truly understand the message of the Gospels. This theology, which seeks to narrow the gap between rich and poor, was embraced by many priests in Latin America and led to their support of trade union movements, political struggles, and protests that aided the poor.

Although not all Latin American priests embraced liberation theology, some took the more radical approach, despite the threats and the danger. Many became victims of right-wing death squads, including Oscar Romero, archbishop of El Salvador. These courageous people did not die in vain; their deaths helped galvanize support among Catholics interested in human rights all over the world.

Today, there are many Catholic charities devoted to peacemaking, both internationally and within specific communities. Development and Peace, an international Catholic organization, works in war-ravaged areas such as Afghanistan, East Timor, and the Congo. The U.S. bishops issued a Call to Solidarity with Africa to focus attention on the problems of the continent and have also made statements on Israeli-Palestinian violence. The Catholic Campaign for Human Development is conducting an awareness campaign about poverty in America.

The Church also keeps a close watch on scientific discoveries through its committee on Science and Human Values, which identifies areas in which ethical discussion is necessary to advance the common good. The committee enters into dialogue with scientists to understand new developments and isolate ethical issues, and it has issued public statements about topics such as global population, genetic testing, genetic screening, death and dying, cloning, stem cell research, genetic modification in plants, evolution, and the relationship of brain, mind, and spirit.

The Holy See has a representative in Washington, D.C., and at the United Nations in New York. The U.S. bishops take prominent stands on public issues and make presentations to government committees on topics as diverse as reproductive technology, the economy, the environment, and the arms race. Although the Church's opposition to reproductive choice led to its stance against legislation to improve the equality of women, including the Equal Rights Amendment, lay Catholic organizations have not hesitated to press the feminist cause and other liberal causes. Lay organizations represent a range of political views and lobby in a wider spectrum of issues than do the bishops. These organizations champion causes such as homosexual rights, the peace movement, racial equality, social justice, and international development.

Ultimately, whichever course of action is taken, Catholics are called to devote time and money to causes that improve the world and the life of those in it. Good works are not only a requirement of Catholic life and a route to unity with Jesus, they also provide the opportunity to work for justice and equality on a political stage.

∾ 101 ∾

DIALOGUE WITH OTHER FAITHS

The Decree on Ecumenism, passed by Vatican II, urges fellow Christians to have brotherly generosity toward one another. Because of Vatican II, the Church began a movement toward ecumenical dialogue and greater understanding among Catholics and people who practice other religions.

Although the Church continues to assert that it is the one true religion, it also acknowledges that God may make His grace known to other peoples of the world who have not yet embraced the truths of Catholicism.

The U.S. branch of the Church established a Commission for Ecumenical Affairs, which met for the first time in March 1965. It appointed personnel to begin making contact with Lutheran, Anglican, Presbyterian, and other Protestant denominations. The commission joined the Division of Christian Unity of the National Council of the Churches of Christ in the United States and the Commission on Faith and Order of the National Council. It also began dialogue with various branches of the Eastern, or Orthodox, churches. Eventually, this ecumenical dialogue would grow to encompass relations with Jewish, Muslim, Buddhist, and other non-Christian communities.

The commission was renamed the Bishops' Committee for Ecumenical and Interreligious Affairs in 1966. It currently has nineteen bishops serving as members and consultants, and more than ninety Catholic theologians and other experts participate in the ongoing dialogues and consultations. Worldwide, the Church participates in the World Council of Churches through the Pontifical Council for Promoting Christian Unity for the Catholic Church.

The shared Gospel of Jesus Christ unites all Christians. The Church already shares many values and sacraments with other Christian religions. It is keen to work with other Christians on issues of social justice and morality, and on spreading the gospel message, and it has held in-depth discussions on scripture, salvation, sanctification, and the Eucharist.

Some of these discussions, such as the dialogue with the Anglican Church, resulted in much common ground. With some other faiths, such as the Southern Baptists, there are larger areas of disagreement, but dialogue has resulted in an understanding of one another's position.

A 1991 dialogue from the World Council of Churches resulted in a document outlining areas of agreement on the Eucharist. The eventual goal is to reach an understanding on how to share in a common communion, including experiencing the Eucharist together.

The Church believes that unity will be accomplished through prayer, discussion, and new understandings among the Christian churches. Almost all Christian churches are, in fact, participating in this movement toward ecumenism. In practice, they have come together in Christian charities, peace, and social justice movements to work toward a common cause. But there is still a long way to go toward a time when all Christians can share communion.

The Church believes that respect and love must also be shown to non-Christians and their faiths. Those who serve one God, such as Muslims and Jews, have much in common with Christians. From Buddhism and Hinduism, Christians can learn techniques of meditation and other skills that will bring them closer to God. The institutional Church has official dialogues set up with leaders of these religions, and it even has a mandate to talk with nonbelievers as well.

Timeline of Key Events:
Hinduism, Judaism, Christianity, Buddhism, and Islam

c. 1500–1200 B.C.: Rig-Veda Hymns written

c. 1300–1200 B.C.: Vedantism

c. 1230–1240 B.C.: Moses leads the Israelites out of bondage

1077–1037 B.C.: King David rules Israel

1027–997 B.C.: King Solomon rules Israel

c. 925: Israel splits into two states: Israel and Judah

858 B.C.: Elijah becomes a prophet of God

c. 850–750 B.C.: Brahmanism

739 B.C.: Isaiah is a prophet of God

722 B.C.: Israel falls to Assyria

c. 720 B.C.: Brahmanas written

c. 700 B.C.: Time of Shramanas (religious wanderers)

c. 600 B.C.: Aranyakas written

596 B.C.: Judah falls to Babylon

528 B.C.: Judeans return from Babylonian captivity

c. 560–480 B.C.: The life of Buddha (Siddhartha Gautama)

c. 509 B.C.: Israel and Judah fall under control of the Roman Empire

c. 500 B.C.: Hinduism

c. 479 B.C.: First council results in four Buddhist factions

c. 469 B.C.: Approximately sixteen Buddhist factions exist

c. 390 B.C.: Second Council declares Buddhist minority orthodox
(Hinayana) and majority heretic (Mahayana)

c. 300 B.C.: Tantras written down

c. 300 B.C.: Buddhism arrives in Sri Lanka

300 B.C.–A.D. 30: Era of Sadducees, Essenes, Samaritans, Zealots, and Pharisees (precursors to Rabbinic Judaism)

297 B.C.: King Asoka converts to Buddhism; Buddhism grows from a small group to a major world religion, as Asoka sends out missionaries

247 B.C.: Asoka calls Third Council to agree on authentic Buddhist scriptures

200 B.C.–200 A.D.: Development of Hinayana Buddhism:

c. 50 B.C.: Buddhism arrives in China: Mahayana tradition develops

37 B.C.: Herod captures Jerusalem

4 B.C.–A.D. 30: Life of Jesus (begins his ministry A.D. 27)

A.D. 30: Pentecost: The birth of the Christian Church

30–600: The early Christian Church

35: Conversion of Saul, who becomes St. Paul

35–312: Age of Martyrs

42: Antioch is the center of Christian activity

c. 50: Vaishnavism

c. 64: Peter and Paul martyred in Rome

69: Bishop Ignatius consecrated in Antioch (St. Peter was the first bishop there; other early bishops of Antioch include James, Polycarp, and Clement)

c. 70: Saivism

70: Destruction of the Temple of Jerusalem

66–73: First Jewish War against Rome

c. 70–110: New Testament Gospels are written

99: Death of St. Clement, first Bishop of Rome and successor to St. Peter

c. 100: Composition of Bhagavad-Gita

100–200: As many as 500 Buddhist sects exist

150: St. Justin Martyr describes liturgical worship of the Church, centered in the Eucharist

132–135: Second Jewish War

c. 200: Laws of Manu compiled

200–300: Development of Mahayana Buddhism

300: Buddhism arrives in Japan

313: Constantine, emperor or Rome, embraces Christianity; Edict of Milan stops persecution of Christians (Constantine is not baptized until shortly before his death many years later)

320–600: Vajrayana Buddhism develops

325: The Nicene Creed is created at the Council of Bishops at Nicaea (the first of seven Ecumenical Councils)

330: Foundation of Constantinople

354–430: Life of St. Augustine of Hippo

381: First Council of Constantinople; Emperor Theodosius declares Christianity official religion of Roman Empire

387–493: Life of St. Patrick

397: Bishops at Carthage formalize New Testament

400: Completion of Jerusalem Talmud

400–600: Rise of Pure Land sects in China

410: Fall of Rome

451: Council of Chalcedon affirms apostolic doctrine of dual nature of Christ

c. 480–547: Life of St. Benedict, founder of Benedictine order

480: Bodhidharma goes to China as a Buddhist missionary

c. 500: Hindu Tantric tradition established

530: Founding of Benedictine order; the Benedictine Rule of monastic life served as the first constitution for monastic life and gave rise to other, subsequent Catholic monastic orders.

538–597: Zhi-yi's life (founder of Tiantai)

c. 550: Tiantai school of Buddhism develops

553: Second Council of Constantinople

570–632: Life of Muhammad

447: A synod in Toledo, Spain, adds the filoque to the Nicene Creed, which asserts that the Holy Spirit proceeds from the Father and the Son

590–604: Pope Gregory I

c. 600: Beginning of Bhakti movement

c. 600–700: Shiah and Sufi branches of Islam develop

600–1300: Papal rule

638: Muslim conquest of Jerusalem

c. 640: Buddhism spreads to Tibet

c. 650: Tantrayana tradition, a radical reinterpretation of Mahayana Buddhism, develops

c. 650–750: Nara schools of Buddhism develop in Japan

691: Dome of the Rock built in Jerusalem

c. 700: Tendai school of Buddhism develops in Japan

711: Muslims begin to conquer Spain

732: Charles Martel halts Arab advance near Poitiers

749: First Buddhist monastery established in Tibet

c. 750: Development of Sephardic Judaism

787: Second Council of Nicaea, ending the era of Ecumenical Councils—restores the use of icons to the Church

800–1806: Holy Roman Empire

880: Photian Schism between Rome and Constantinople

c. 900–1300: Second revival of Buddhism in Tibet

c. 950–1000: Conversion of Europe to Christianity is completed

988: Conversion of Russia

c. 1000: Sunni branch of Islam develops

c. 1000s: Reform of Tantric tradition

c. 1000–1200: India encounters Islam; iconoclasm:

1054: Great Schism: Roman Catholic and Eastern Orthodox Churches split

1071: Battle of Manzikert

1073: Pope Gregory VII centralizes control of Church with new theory of papal superiority

1095–1254: The Crusades

c. 1150: Ashkenazic Judaism develops

c. 1150: Zen Buddhism develops in Japan

c. 1200s: Pure Land, Nichiren, and Zen sects develop in Japan

c. 1200s: Decline of Buddhism in Northern India

1204: Sack of Constantinople

1212: St. Francis creates the first of the mendicant orders, the Franciscans. Dominicans, Carmelites, and Augustinians also arise in the 1200s.

1224–1274: Life of St. Thomas Aquinas

1231–1834: The Inquisitions

c. 1250: Nichiren Buddhism develops in Japan

1291: Muslims seize Acre

1333: St. Gregory Palamas defends Orthodox practice of Hesychast spirituality (a form of Eastern monasticism) and the use of the Jesus prayer

1350–1700: European Renaissance

1377–1407: Great Papal Schism (struggle between Rome and Avignon)

1391–1475: Life of Dge-'Dun-Grub, first Dalai Lama

c. 1400s: Decline of Buddhism in Southern India

1469–c. 1539: life of Nanak, Indian religious leader who broke from orthodox Hinduism and founded Sikhism

1453: Muslims seize Constantinople; end of Byzantine Empire

1483–1546: Life of Martin Luther

1492: Fall of Grenada

c. 1500s: Muslim influence on Hinduism

1509–64: John Calvin's life

1517: Martin Luther nails his 96 Theses to the door of the Roman Church in Wittenberg

1517–1648: Protestant Reformation

c. 1523: Lutheran Church develops *

c. 1525: Anabaptists (leads to Mennonite and Amish)

1529: Church of England begins separation from Rome

c. 1534: Episcopalian: Henry VIII's Act of Supremacy

c. 1536: Calvinism

1540: Formation of the Jesuits

1542–1648: Catholic Counter-Reformation

1544: Jesuit missionary work begins in Japan, Africa, and North America

1545–63: Roman Catholic Council of Trent

1559: John Calvin sends missionaries throughout Europe to convert Catholics to the new faith of Protestantism

c. 1560: Presbyterian

c. 1564: Puritan

1566: Pope Pius V standardizes Latin Mass

c. 1600: Sikhism

c. 1609: Baptist

1627–82: Reign of Ngag-Dbang-Blo-Bzang Rgya-Mtsho, "Great Fifth" Dalai Lama

c. 1647: Quaker

1697–1790: The Enlightenment

1700–60: Life of Yisra'El Ben Eli'ezer

c. 1700: Hasidic Judaism develops

c. 1700: Khalsa

1709–91: Life of John Wesley

c.: 1738: Methodist

1760–1914: The Industrial Revolution

1782: First publication of Philokalia, a classic of spirituality

c. 1784: Shakers

1789: Protestant Episcopalian (U.S.)

1789: First Roman Catholic bishop (John Carrol) in the United States, and first diocese (the See of Baltimore)

1794: Introduction of Orthodoxy to North America when missionaries arrive on Kodiak Island in Alaska

c. 1830: Book of Mormon by John Smith

1832: Church of Christ

1845–48: Sikh Wars

c. 1849: Adventist

1854: Roman Catholic Dogma of Immaculate Conception

1863: Baha'i

1863: Seventh Day Adventist

1869–70: First Vatican Council; Roman Catholic dogma of Papal Infallibility

1869–72: St. Nicholas establishes Japanese Mission

1869–1948: Life of Mohandas Ghandi

1870: Jehovah's Witnesses

1892: Church of Christ Scientist

1897: Zionist movement

1901: Pentecostal

1920s: Soviet Communism attack on Buddhism in Mongolia

1930: Nation of Islam (U.S.)

1933–45: The Holocaust

1932: Saudi Arabia established

1945: Nag Hammadi Library discovered in Egypt

1948: State of Israel established

1950: Chinese communism attack on Buddhism

1952: World Fellowship of Buddhists formed

1962–65: Second Vatican Council

1988: 1,000-year anniversary of Orthodoxy in Russia

1989: First woman ordained in Episcopal church

2000: Roman Catholic Jubilee

*Note: The branches of Protestantism mentioned in this timeline are by no means intended to be a comprehensive representation of all Protestant denominations. (At present, more than 500 Protestant denominations exist in the United States alone.) These denominations are meant to paint a fairly broad picture of some primary Protestant groupings, from which many other denominations stem. For more detailed information, refer to *www.laymanswalk.org/magazine/2002/2002.shtml*.

Sources: *The World Almanac*, 1998; *Encyclopedia Britannica, 15th Edition*, 1993; *The World's Religions*, Smart, 1998; *Illustrated Guide to World Religions*, Coogan, 1998; *World Religions from Ancient History to Present*, Parrinder, 1985; Conciliar Press, 1998; *Catholic Bible Apologetics, 1985–1997*.